Reading Comprehension

LinguiSystems Staff

Skill Areas:	Reading Comprehension Language
Ages:	10 through 13
Grades:	5 through 8

LinguiSystems, Inc.
3100 4th Avenue
East Moline, IL 61244-9700
1-800-PRO IDEA
1-800-776-4332

FAX: 1-800-577-4555
E-mail: service@linguisystems.com
Web: www.linguisystems.com
TDD: 1-800-933-8331
(for those with hearing impairments)

Copyright © 2002 LinguiSystems, Inc.

All of our products are copyrighted to protect the fine work of our authors. You may only copy the worksheets as needed for your own use with students. Any other reproduction or distribution of the pages in this book is prohibited, including copying the entire book to use as another primary source or "master" copy.

Printed in the U.S.A.

ISBN 0-7606-0471-1

About the Authors

Carolyn LoGiudice, Rosemary Huisingh, Lauri Whiskeyman, Barb Truman, Linda Bowers, Paul F. Johnson

This spirited group of educators and writers at LinguiSystems collaborated to develop *Strategic Learning: Reading Comprehension, Level 2*. Together we have many years of experience educating and working with students to improve their language and reading skills. As LinguiSystems employees, we share a zest for life and a passion for high-quality education for all students. We hope the materials we develop reflect our philosophy.

Cover design by Mike Paustian

Original illustrations by Margaret Warner and Paul Dallgas-Frey

Clip art and photographs © 2002 www.arttoday.com

Table of Contents

Introduction 5

Main Idea 7

Sequencing 19

Context Clues 33

Predicting 48

Cause and Effect 62

Referents 72

Comparing and Contrasting 87

Fact and Opinion 104

Summarizing 114

Inferences 126

Figurative Language 141

Imagery 156

Answer Key 167

Introduction

Strategic Learning: Reading Comprehension, Level 2 offers time-tested, practical strategies that help all students take an active role in understanding and thinking about what they read. This program does not address phonics or word attack skills; it assumes students can decode material at a grade level of 3.0-6.0 (Flesch-Kincaid readability scale). The activities focus on the most critical reading and comprehension skills taught in major language arts texts. These critical skills help students to integrate listening, understanding, thinking, speaking, and writing as they approach written material.

The skill areas targeted in the units of this program are arranged by order of the cognitive complexity required to understand and execute the tasks within the units. The student activity worksheets for each unit are also sequenced in order of difficulty. Select the activities most appropriate for your students. Present each unit in sequence or select skill areas to supplement other curricular materials.

Each unit begins with instructor information listing the goal(s) and objectives for that unit. Enrichment activities are also offered for supplemental instruction. These activities help your students to continue learning and to master the unit objectives. A specific goal for each activity worksheet is listed in a box at the top of each page.

The first student page in each unit gives students a chance to preview the strategy they will be learning. Present these pages to your students in a discussion format. Have your students keep these overviews in personal folders for their reference throughout the year. Encourage your students to paraphrase the information to demonstrate their understanding of the strategies. Review the specific strategy steps or questions before you present specific worksheets to your students.

Research proves that repeated readings improve reading comprehension and that three readings are usually sufficient repetition to grasp content, assuming the text is at or below a student's reading level. We recommend training students to read a passage three times for adequate comprehension of expository text. Apply this systematic approach throughout the activities in this program for maximum benefit.

As you teach one skill, you may also have the chance to highlight other critical skills for reading comprehension. For example, as you teach about identifying the main idea, you may encounter opportunities to address inferring, predicting, and

Introduction, *continued*

summarizing. Take advantage of these opportunities, if doing so would not distract your students from the featured skill area, to help students appreciate the complex process of reading for understanding.

Many of the activities in this book cross the curriculum and work well with large, diverse classrooms as well as with individual students. For whole classrooms or large groups, make overheads of the student worksheets to model the skills and strategies easily for your students.

Answers for most of the student worksheets are listed in the answer key at the back of the book. In many cases, the answers are merely examples of appropriate responses. Accept other logical responses as correct.

No reading comprehension program can teach all students to understand what they read or to be active readers. The strategic approach in this resource is appropriate for most students, especially those with reading or language-based difficulties. The key factor for success with this material, though, is the same as for any other program—the instructor. Modeling your own reading comprehension strategies sends a powerful message to your students. Adapt this instruction material as you see fit, and present it in your own professional style that considers your unique students. We hope you find this book a welcome resource that helps students perceive meaning and derive satisfaction from whatever they read.

Linda, Rosemary, Paul, Carolyn, Barb, and Lauri

Main Idea

> **Goal:** to identify the main ideas and supporting details in reading passages
>
> **Objectives:** In this unit, your students will:
>
> - identify the main idea and supporting details in reading passages
> - find details that support the main idea of a paragraph
> - understand and identify the topic, main idea, and details of a passage
> - understand the difference between a stated main idea and an unstated main idea
> - understand the difference between supporting and non-supporting details

Finding the main idea of a reading passage requires students to evaluate information and make judgments based on what they have read. For reading success, students need to understand what *main idea* and *detail* mean. Students also need to know that supporting details in a reading passage will help them identify the main idea.

In this unit, students will learn to identify the main idea and details of a reading passage. They will also identify supporting and non-supporting details in a variety of reading passages. Knowing the main idea of a reading passage will improve students' grasp of what they read.

Enrichment Activities

1. Before reading a book aloud, show students the cover of the book. Talk about the title and the picture. To find the topic, ask questions, such as "What do you think this story will be about?" or "What does the picture tell you?" To find the main idea, start reading the story, but stop periodically to talk about the main idea of a chapter or section. As you read the story, encourage students to point out details that support the main idea. Write the main idea on the board and list the details beneath it.

2. Ask students to find the main ideas and details of bulletin board displays, school announcements, advertisements, and popular songs.

Main Idea, continued

> Instructor Information

3. Give students a way to find and remember the main idea and supporting details as they read. A graphic organizer such as the one below can be helpful.

   Main Idea (What is this paragraph about?) _____

   _____

   Supporting Details

   1. _____
   2. _____
   3. _____
   ---

4. Newspaper articles are a great source for a variety of reading passages for students. Have them read the headlines and make predictions about what the articles will be about. Then have them read the articles to see if their predictions are right. Are the headlines the main idea of the articles? Have them work in pairs or alone to find the main idea and supporting details of the articles.

5. As students read short stories, have them pause after one or two paragraphs. Ask questions to stimulate their thinking, such as "What is the main idea of the paragraph you just read?" or "What was the paragraph about?" Next have the students work in small groups or pairs to ask their own questions and talk about the main ideas of paragraphs they have read. Finally have students read independently, pause after one or two paragraphs, and ask themselves about the main idea of the passage.

6. Have students talk about a TV show or movie they have seen. Encourage them to describe the plot in just one sentence (the main idea). For fun, watch a short video or DVD in class and have students write down the main idea (plot). Once they have written a sentence that tells the main idea, have them paraphrase it to reinforce the concept of *main idea*.

7. When students choose library books, have them give oral reports that tell what the book is about. Have them identify the overall main idea of the book.

8. When students are reading a chapter book or a textbook, encourage them to look for clues like bold headings, chapter titles, graphic elements, and photos to identify the main idea and details.

Main Idea

> Goal: identify the main idea and supporting details of a passage

The **main idea** is what a paragraph or story is about. To figure out the main idea, ask yourself, "What is this paragraph or story about?"

Dr. Whoo has invented many things. He invented an electric fork to warm each bite. He invented a machine to tie your shoes. He even invented root-beer toothpaste. What will he think of next?

What is this story about? *Dr. Whoo's inventions*

Sometimes a writer states the **main idea** in a **topic sentence**. Other times you have to figure out the main idea by looking at the other sentences in the paragraph.

Sentences that tell more about the main idea are called **supporting details**. The other sentences are called **non-supporting details**. They don't relate directly to the main idea.

To understand what you read, follow these steps.

◆ Look for a **topic sentence** that tells you what the paragraph or story is about.

◆ If you can't find a topic sentence, ask yourself, "What is this paragraph about?"

◆ Another way to figure out the main idea is to pretend that you have to tell someone what the paragraph is about in one sentence. What would you say? Your answer is the **main idea**.

◆ If you still can't tell what the main idea is, look at the other sentences in the paragraph. Decide which ones are the **supporting details**. What are these details talking about? That's the main idea.

Strategic Learning
Reading Comprehension: Level 2

Main Idea

Goal: Identify the main idea in a paragraph

Read each paragraph. Check the sentence that tells the main idea for each one.

1. A symbol is a thing that stands for something else. This  is a symbol. It stands for poison. A heart  is a symbol that stands for love. This  symbol tells you that there is a hospital nearby.

    a. ____ Some signs tell you about traffic.
    b. ____ A symbol is a thing that stands for something else.
    c. ____ All symbols stand for the same thing.

2. A flag stands for the people, land, and beliefs of a country. The United States' flag has 50 stars. Each star stands for one of the 50 states. This flag also has 13 stripes. Each stripe stands for one of the first 13 colonies.

    a. ____ The United States has 50 states.
    b. ____ The United States' flag has stars and stripes.
    c. ____ A flag stands for the people, land, and beliefs of a country.

3. The Statue of Liberty is a symbol of freedom. She stands in New York Harbor. She welcomes all ships that enter it. She holds her torch high to show that the United States is a free country.

    a. ____ The Statue of Liberty is in New York Harbor.
    b. ____ The Statue of Liberty is a symbol of freedom.
    c. ____ The Statue of Liberty holds a torch in one hand.

Main Idea

Goal: Identify the main idea of a newspaper article

The headline of a newspaper article usually tells the main idea of the article. Read each article. Then choose the best headline.

1. Daniel Woods, a fifth-grader from Kent, won the state spelling bee. He outspelled 34 other students to win. His winning word was *affable*. Daniel will go to the national spelling bee next month.

   a. ____ Spelling Bees Are Fun

   b. ____ 5th Grader Wins State Spelling Bee

   c. ____ Winning a Spelling Bee

2. One hundred fishermen turned out for the start of the annual fishing contest held at Clear Lake. The contest runs for two months. Any fish caught during this time will be measured for weight and length. The person with the largest catch wins one year's supply of bait. Updates will be published weekly.

   a. ____ Fish Tales

   b. ____ Fishing Around

   c. ____ Annual Fishing Contest Begins

3. This winter, we have gotten more snow than usual. More than six feet of snow have fallen and winter isn't over yet. Last year at this time, we only had a couple of inches of snow. Cold winds from the north are thought to be causing the increased snow.

   a. ____ Old Man Winter

   b. ____ Is It Spring Yet?

   c. ____ More Snow Than Usual

4. The school board has voted to give $1000 to each school in the city. Each school can decide how to spend the money. There are no strings attached. Principal John Stone of Wilson School is grateful. "We need new music stands for the music department. This money has come at the right time."

   a. ____ Extra Money for Schools

   b. ____ Money for Music

   c. ____ School Board Votes

Strategic Learning
Reading Comprehension: Level 2

Main Idea

Goal: Identify the main idea in a paragraph

Read each paragraph about the Civil War. Check the sentence that states the main idea.

1. The North and South fought the First Battle of Bull Run near Washington, D.C. The North was sure they would win. They even invited people to come watch! Hundreds of people came. Some even brought picnic lunches to eat as they watched the fight. But surprise! The South won the battle. The scared sightseers quickly went home.

    a. ____ The First Battle of Bull Run was near Washington, D.C.

    b. ____ It was a surprise when the South won the battle.

    c. ____ Hundreds of people came to watch the First Battle of Bull Run.

2. When the Civil War began, many men left their homes to go fight. They left behind their families and their jobs. The men were gone, but someone still needed to do their work. Up until that time, women had worked mainly in their homes. Now they took over the men's jobs. Some women worked in the fields. Some women worked in factories. Some women ran businesses. Other women became nurses and took care of wounded soldiers. Some women even became spies.

    a. ____ During the Civil War, women took over the jobs the men had left behind.

    b. ____ Many men left their homes to fight in the Civil War.

    c. ____ Women worked in their homes during the Civil War.

3. During the Civil War, runaway slaves used a secret route to escape to the North. This secret route was called the Underground Railroad. It was not a real railroad and it was not below the ground. It was the path slaves took to freedom. They mostly traveled at night. They hid during the day so they wouldn't be caught. When they reached the North, many went to Canada. They were safe there.

    a. ____ The Underground Railroad was not underground or a railroad.

    b. ____ The Underground Railroad helped runaway slaves travel to freedom.

    c. ____ Runaway slaves went to Canada.

Main Idea

Goal: Identify supporting details of a paragraph

Pretend you are going to write a paragraph about each main idea. Check off each sentence you could use as a supporting detail in your paragraph. Choose only the details that apply directly to the main idea.

1. Main Idea: how an ostrich protects itself

    a. _____ An ostrich uses its speed to escape from its enemies.
    b. _____ An ostrich would suffocate if it buried its head in the sand.
    c. _____ Ostriches use their sharp, thick nails as weapons.
    d. _____ An ostrich uses its strong legs to kick its enemy.
    e. _____ Ostriches are only found in Africa.

2. Main Idea: the three kinds of blood vessels

    a. _____ Your heart is a pump that pushes blood throughout your body.
    b. _____ Arteries are blood vessels that carry blood away from your heart.
    c. _____ Veins carry blood from your capillaries to your heart.
    d. _____ Red blood cells give blood its color.
    e. _____ Capillaries are tiny blood vessels that connect your arteries and your veins.

3. Main Idea: making cornflakes

    a. _____ Cornflakes start as kernels cut from a corncob.
    b. _____ The kernels are ground into hominy and cooked over steam.
    c. _____ Many people eat cornflakes for breakfast.
    d. _____ Cornflakes are best when strawberries are put on them.
    e. _____ When the hominy is dry, it is broken into flakes and roasted.

4. Main Idea: safety rules for electricity

    a. _____ Don't plug too many things into one outlet.
    b. _____ Don't use an electrical appliance when you are wet or standing in water.
    c. _____ You can buy light bulbs at many different stores.
    d. _____ Your electricity may go out during a bad storm.
    e. _____ Stay away from power lines.

Main Idea

Goal: Identify supporting details in a paragraph

Read each paragraph. Underline the details in the paragraph that support the main idea.

1. Main Idea: facts about sloth bears

    Sloth bears are very active and very brave, too. They climb trees to gather honey right from the beehive. Their long, shaggy fur looks messy, but sloth bear cubs can easily hang from their mothers' backs while they travel around the forest.

2. Main Idea: how animals keep warm in winter

    When it gets cold out, animals stay warm in different ways. Some animals go to warmer areas. Some animals just go to sleep until spring. Other animals fluff up their fur or feathers. Some small animals, like bees, huddle into a tight ball to keep each other warm.

3. Main Idea: how fireworks work

    Fireworks have two kinds of gunpowder. The powder is packed into a paper tube called a *rocket*. When you light the fuse, one kind of gunpowder starts to burn. This makes the rocket go up. When the rocket is high in the sky, the heat sets fire to the rest of the gunpowder. The rocket explodes, creating colorful designs in the sky.

4. Main Idea: Space Camp helps you learn about space travel.

    Space Camp is for anyone who wants to be an astronaut. Campers stay for five days. They hear lectures, watch films, tour a space flight center, and launch model rockets. The best part is a simulated space shuttle mission. They launch the shuttle, fix a satellite, and land. Space Camp is a great way to learn about space travel.

Main Idea

Goal: Identify supporting details and main idea of a paragraph

Read each ad. Underline all the supporting details about the product. Then check the main idea.

1. It's a scooter! It's a skateboard! Take off the handle and the Scoot-n-Skate is a skateboard. Put the handle back on and you've got a scooter. It's easy to use and it comes in lots of colors.

   Get the Scoot-n-Skate today!

   It's 2 toys in 1!

   a. ____ the colors Scoot-n-Skates come in
   b. ____ riding a Scoot-n-Skate
   c. ____ how a Scoot-n-Skate works

2.  What do books, computers, and fun have in common? You can find them all at the Dayton Public Library. We get new books weekly. We have monthly reading contests, too! And you can play the latest games on our computers. We know you'll have fun at the library!

   a. ____ having fun at the Dayton Public Library
   b. ____ reading books at the Dayton Public Library
   c. ____ studying at the Dayton Public Library

3. Got cold feet? Then you'll love our battery-operated warming socks. These cozy socks will keep your toes warm, even on the coldest days. Just one AAA battery in each sock will keep your feet warm for up to 24 hours. Only $12.95. One size fits most. Call now and you'll get an extra pair free! And don't forget to ask about our hats and mittens!

   a. ____ winter clothing
   b. ____ using batteries to stay warm
   c. ____ battery-operated warming socks

Strategic Learning
Reading Comprehension: Level 2

15

Copyright © 2002 LinguiSystems, Inc.

Main Idea

Goal: Identify the main idea and supporting details of a paragraph

Read each paragraph about Indian homes. Write each main idea. Underline three details that tell about each main idea.

1. Navajo families needed homes that were good for desert living. They lived in hogans. Hogans were mound-like buildings made from mud and logs. The mud walls kept the hogans cool in summer and warm in winter. Hogans did not have windows. They had one door that faced east, toward the rising sun. They also had a hole in the roof to let out smoke from a fire.

   Main Idea: _____

2. The Cheyenne needed homes they could put up and take down in a hurry. They lived in tepees. Tepees are cone-shaped tents. The Cheyenne tied long wooden poles together at the top. They spread out the bottom of the poles to make a circle. They sewed animal hides together. Then they stretched the hides over the wooden poles. Sometimes they painted pictures on the outside of their tepees. To keep warm, they built a fire in the center of the tepee. The smoke went out a small hole at the top of the tepee.

   Main Idea: _____

16
Copyright © 2002 LinguiSystems, Inc.

Strategic Learning
Reading Comprehension: Level 2

Main Idea

Goal: Identify the main idea and supporting details of a paragraph

Read each paragraph. Write the main idea on the line. Underline the supporting details that tell about the main idea.

1. If you see a black spider with a red hourglass shape on its stomach, stay away from it! It's a black widow spider, one of the deadliest animals around. Its bite is very painful. If one bites you, you will start to feel bad within an hour. You will get a bad headache and be sick to your stomach. Your muscles may start to go into spasms. You could die from a black widow's bite. If one bites you, get help right away.

   Main Idea: _____

2. How do mosquitoes choose the people they bite? Mosquitoes like moist skin. If your skin is soft and moist, they may enjoy taking a few bites of you. They are also drawn to the carbon dioxide in your breath when you exhale. And they like the chemicals in your sweat. If you have lactic acid in your body, mosquitoes will love you, too. They only bite the tastiest people!

   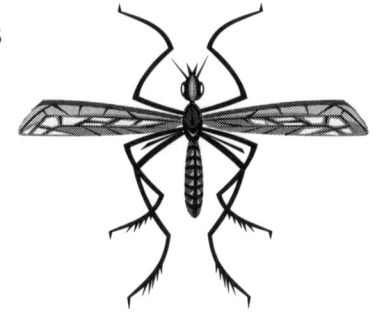

   Main Idea: _____

3. Roaches are pesky bugs that help themselves to your home and your food. If you see one roach at home, you probably have hundreds more hiding. It's very hard to get rid of them. On the other hand, these pests are good for medical research. Some doctors use them to study heart disease. Other doctors use them for cancer research. Doctors also use roaches to learn things about the human brain.

   Main Idea: _____

Strategic Learning
Reading Comprehension: Level 2

Main Idea

Goal: Identify the main idea and non-supporting details of a paragraph

Read each paragraph. Underline the main idea. Then draw a line through each non-supporting detail. There are two non-supporting details in each passage.

1. If everyone helped, we could clean up the litter around our school in less than an hour. Then our school would look much better. We could bring big garbage bags. There are some in the supply room. We could pick up the trash, bag it, and throw it in the dumpster. The dumpster is never full because it is emptied twice a week.

2. There was a break-in last week at Hayes Elementary School. My cousin is in fifth grade there. The vandals got in through a window. At least ten computers, two VCRs, and nine TVs were stolen. Paint was smeared down a hallway. The hallway leads to the gym. Police have no suspects yet.

3. The Knox County Sheriff's Department has lost a best friend, a German shepherd police dog named Rex. Rex died from a virus earlier this month. Rex had been helping officers for over ten years. He was trained to sniff out drugs. He liked to eat hot dogs. A new dog named Jake has replaced Rex. Jake was trained at the same place Rex was.

4. Part of an amusement park ride collapsed on Tuesday. A steel tower that supports a slingshot ride crashed to the ground at Smoky Point Amusement Park. No one was near the tower when it snapped. The park is closed for the winter. The cause has not been determined. There were no strong winds at the time. The park will open again on May 25th.

Sequencing

Instructor Information

> **Goal:** to tell the correct order of pictures or story events
>
> **Objectives:** In this unit, your students will:
> - tell the order of events
> - find and use sequencing words
> - use timelines and flowcharts to sequence events
> - use spatial words to describe things or their locations
> - apply knowledge to make a timeline or flowchart to sequence events

The ability to correctly sequence events or stories requires logical thinking skills. In this unit, your students will learn to tell the sequence of an event in the correct order. They will find and use sequencing words in reading passages. They will learn to transfer information to a timeline or flowchart to clarify meaning. Your students will also learn to understand and use spatial order to describe things. As your students master sequencing skills, their reading comprehension and thinking skills will improve.

Enrichment Activities

1. Use flowcharts, timelines, and other visual sequencing organizers in your classes. In math, for example, show the process of solving an equation with a flowchart. In history, use a timeline to sequence events. Discuss how things would be different if one step were changed.

2. List the sequence words below on the board. Talk about their meanings with your students. Encourage your students to use the list to help find sequencing words as they are reading. Add words your students suggest to the list.

next (to)	first	over	after	in order
then	last	left	second	beginning
above	top	right	third	
below	beside	before	fourth	

Sequencing, continued

3. Find directions from games, gadgets, or unassembled plastic furniture that require a sequence to play or put together. Have your students plot the steps on a flowchart.

4. Use flowcharts and timelines to organize reports or projects with your students. This visual organization will show them when to begin; what assignments are due first, second, and last; and when the final assignment can be brought to school. Students can personalize the charts by adding details they need to help them remember the sequence.

5. Create schedules of events that occur yearly, monthly, weekly, or daily in your school. Make a schedule of vacations, basketball games, daily classes, assemblies, etc.

6. Have each student create personal life timelines. They can highlight major events, such as their first ride in an airplane or a move to a new town. Encourage students to share the events that are most important to them.

7. Create flowcharts with your students to prepare for tests. Sequence the steps they should follow, from reading the material to reviewing the information the night before the test. As they progress through the steps, review their progress, making changes to the sequence as needed.

8. Use timelines to sequence the events in books you read as a class or as your students read for pleasure.

9. Use spatial sequencing to organize your classroom. Ask students to use spatial and sequencing words to describe their classroom, such as *north*, *south*, *east*, *west*, *upper/lower right*, *along the back*, etc. Help your students get started by dividing the room into sections or quarters with specific labels everyone can refer to for this task.

10. Personalize spatial sequencing by asking students to describe the organization of their desks or lockers. Start from front to back, up to down, right to left, etc. Your students might discover a better way to organize their personal space and end the missing assignment dilemma forever!

Sequencing

Goal: sequence events in order

What might make the directions below hard to follow?

    Take out a sheet of paper.
    Pick up your pencil.
    Put your pencil down.
    Write your name.

These directions are impossible to follow because they are in the wrong sequence, or order. Sequencing means putting events in chronological order, the order in which they happened or will happen.

Here are some tips to help you sequence things in chronological order.

 Look for time or transition words like these that tell when the events happened.

morning	afternoon	lunchtime
first	summer	middle
next	last	July 20, 1892

 Tell the events in order. Sequence the items on a timeline or flowchart.

A timeline shows the order of events by putting the dates below the line and events above the correct date.

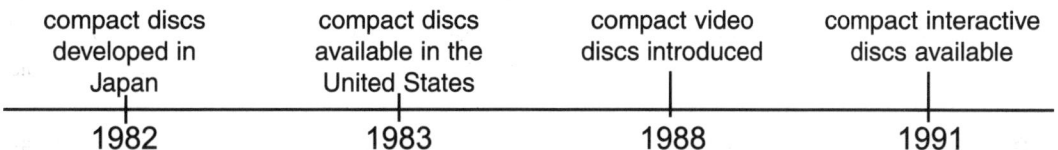

A flowchart is another way to show the sequence of events. It uses arrows to connect events instead of words or dates.

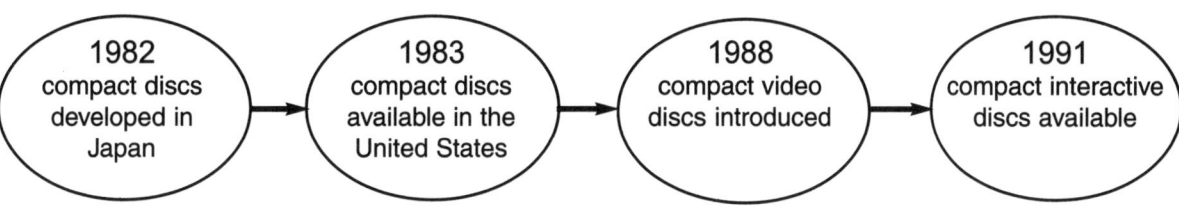

Strategic Learning
Reading Comprehension: Level 2

21

Copyright © 2002 LinguiSystems, Inc.

Sequencing

Goal: Find and use sequence words

Henry's mom asked him to help her around the house. She gave him the following directions. Circle all the sequencing words she used to help Henry do the jobs in the right order.

"Henry, I need your help today," said Mom. "After I leave for work, there are some jobs you can do for me. First take the pie inside and put it on the counter. Then lock the window. At eleven o'clock, turn the sprinkler off. Then put the sprinkler and hose in the garage. Shut and lock the garage door before you leave."

Dave is in a cooking class. He's making his first pizza to share with his friends. Unscramble the directions for him. Number the steps in the correct order. Use the time words to help you.

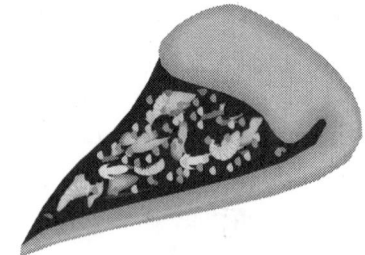

a. ____ Then pour pizza sauce over the dough.

b. ____ Finally bake the pizza at 350 degrees for 20 minutes.

c. ____ Once you have the meat on, sprinkle enough shredded cheese to cover the meat.

d. ____ After the dough and sauce are ready, sauté some sausage and put it on the pizza.

e. ____ First spray the pan lightly with a cooking spray before spreading the dough on the pan.

Sequencing

Goal: Understand and use a timeline

Making a timeline can help you remember facts about people, places, and events. A timeline is organized in chronological order, the order in which the events happened.

Read this passage to help you fill in the timeline below about the history of television.

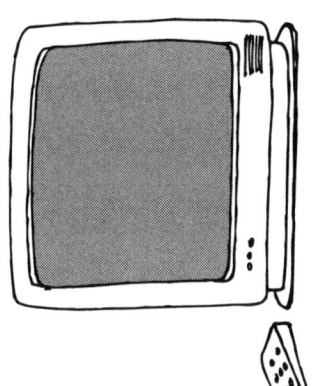

The History of Television

In 1925 a picture was transmitted to a TV screen for the first time. The picture was black and white and there was no sound. Television has come a long way since then.

The National Broadcasting Company, or NBC, started the first TV station in 1930. NBC broadcasted black-and-white TV shows for a few hours each day. It wasn't until 1954 that a color TV show was broadcast nationwide. The first color program was the telecast of the Tournament of Roses Parade. Two years later, in 1956, WNBQ in Chicago became the first TV station to broadcast all shows in color.

TV became a hit in the 1960s. By 1965, 90% of homes in the United States had a television. Almost all shows were in color. Now most people have two or more TVs at home.

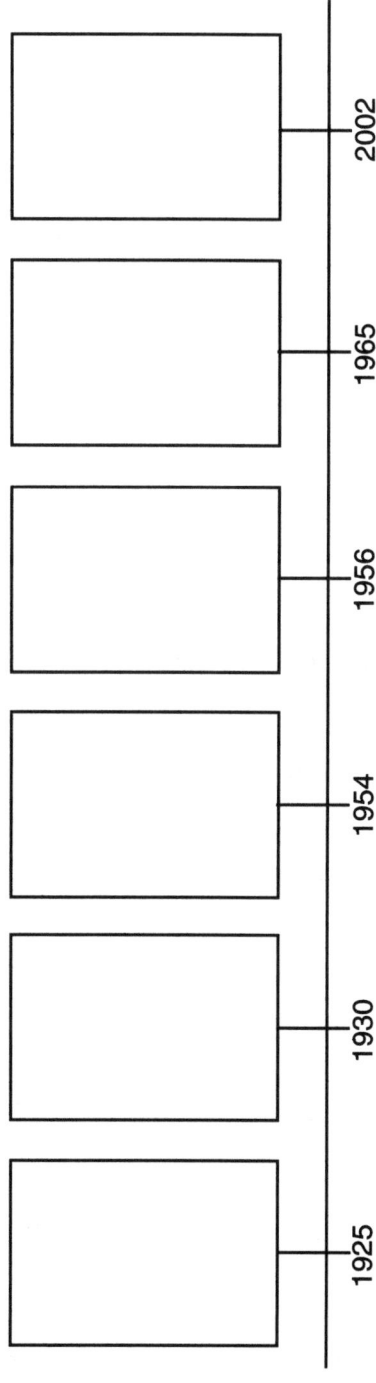

Sequencing

Goal: Understand and use a timeline

Read the passage below. Then create a timeline to put the events in chronological order.

Movie History

Today you can rent or buy movies and show them at home. You can go to the cinemas and see movies on the big screen. If you love movies, you should read about Thomas Edison.

Thomas Edison invented movies. Mr. Edison would be surprised at how they have changed over the years. He invented the movie camera in 1889. About six years later, in 1895, the first movie was shown in Paris, France. It would be another eight years, or 1903, before a movie was made and shown in the United States.

Early movies were made without sound. One of the most famous was *The Great Train Robbery*. It was almost 25 years before sound was added to movies. The first movies with sound came out in 1927. Thomas Edison's invention changed the world.

Here is a list of the events from the movie history passage. Put these events in chronological order on the timeline below.

- Movie rental and purchase available
- First movie shown in Paris
- Sound added to movies
- First movie shown in the U.S.
- Movie camera invented

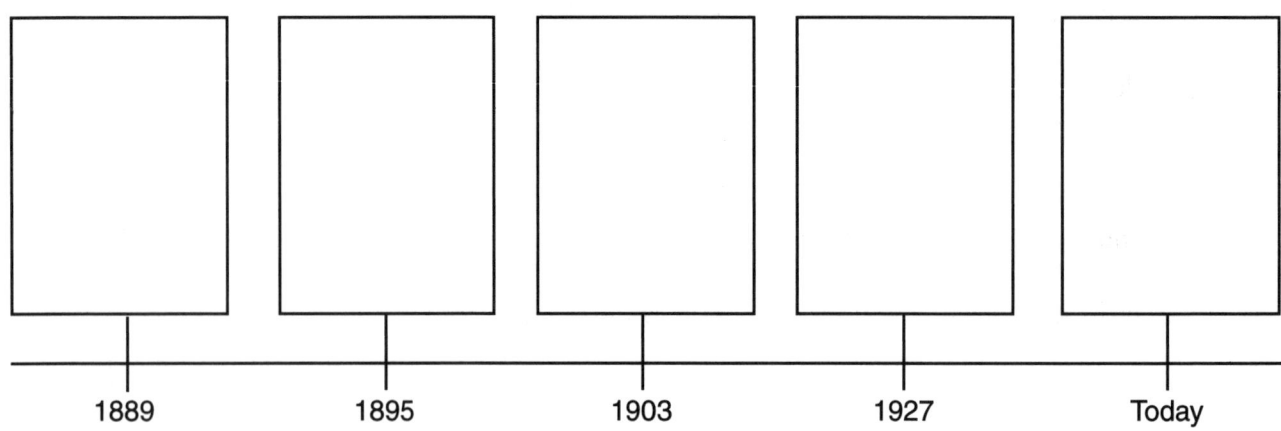

24
Copyright © 2002 LinguiSystems, Inc.

Strategic Learning
Reading Comprehension: Level 2

Sequencing

Goal: Use a timeline to sequence events

Read this story about Mahatma Gandhi. On another sheet of paper, make a time line to record the important events and dates in his life.

Mahatma Gandhi

Mahatma Gandhi was born in India in 1869. Almost from the time he was born, his mother taught him to respect all forms of life and to avoid harming any living thing. Gandhi remembered his mother's words all his life.

Gandhi was married in 1882. He was only 13 years old. By 1891 he was 22 and had finished law school. He tried to practice law in India, but he was shy and he didn't enjoy being a lawyer. In 1893 Gandhi moved to South Africa. There he saw that Indians were mistreated. He spent the next 21 years working for Indians' rights in South Africa.

In 1915 Gandhi went home to India. He began working for the rights of people in India. He taught people nonviolent ways to protest unfair laws. By 1920 he was a great leader and teacher.

On January 30, 1948, Gandhi was shot on his way to a prayer meeting. People all over India and the entire world were sad to lose such a great leader.

Sequencing

Goal: Use a timeline to increase comprehension

Creating a timeline can make it easier to study and remember historical events. Read this paragraph about the invention of communication devices. On a separate sheet of paper, plot each invention on a timeline.

Communication History

It is easy to communicate to friends nowadays. Push a few buttons on a phone and you are connected. An e-mail can zoom across the planet in seconds. Now imagine it is the mid-1800s. You could only talk to friends in person or by letter. The telephone would not be invented for another 30 years, and the computer, why, it was over 100 years away!

Do you know what inventions have changed the way we communicate since the 1800s? The first was the telegraph invented in 1845. It used a code of dots and dashes to spell out a message. The telephone, invented in 1876, let people talk to each other instead of reading a letter written weeks earlier. Thirty years later, in 1906, the first radio brought voices and music through on airwaves. Another 30 years passed before television broadcasted pictures and sound together in 1936. In 1962 the first satellite sent information to us from around the world. During the 1980s, the cellular phone and fax machines were invented. Ten years later, in the 1990s, the Internet was sending information to computers around the world! Video telephones, invented in 2000, let you see your friend as you are talking. What is next and how quickly will it be ready?

Sequencing

Goal: Understand and use a flowchart

A flowchart is another way to show the order of a sequence of events. A flowchart doesn't use time words or dates. It uses arrows instead. Use this flowchart to fill in the blanks for the directions.

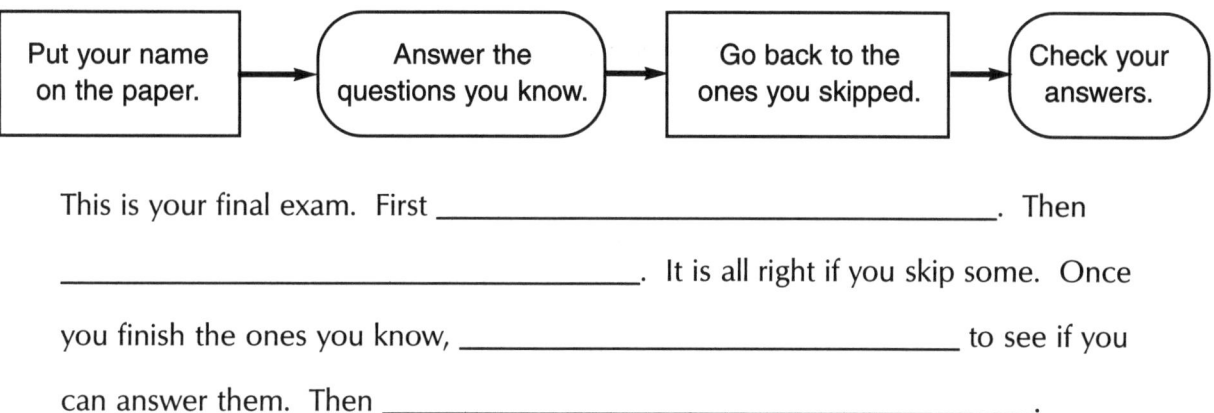

This is your final exam. First _____. Then

_____. It is all right if you skip some. Once

you finish the ones you know, _____ to see if you

can answer them. Then _____.

Flowcharts can also explain how things work or why things happen. Read these sentences that tell about oxygen production plants. Use the information to finish the flowchart.

Plants Help Us Breathe

Did you know that plants help us breathe? We help plants live, too. When we breathe out, we send a gas called **carbon dioxide** into the air. Plants need carbon dioxide to make their food. After they make their food, they send a gas called oxygen into the air. We breathe that oxygen and the cycle starts over again!

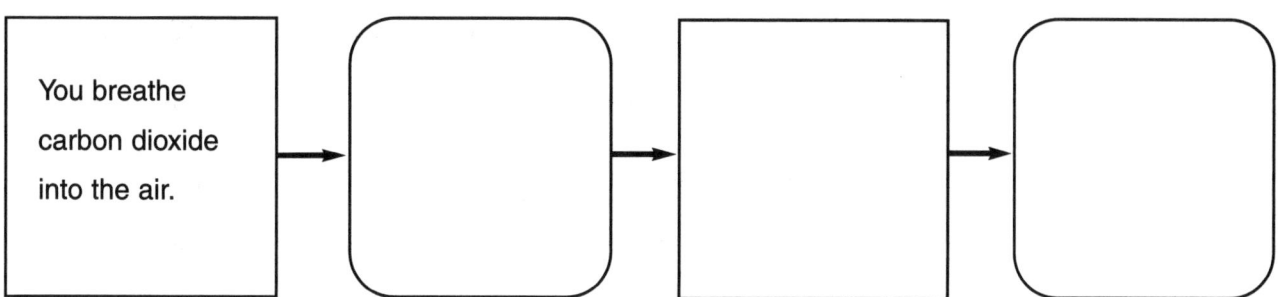

Strategic Learning
Reading Comprehension: Level 2

Sequencing

Goal: Understand and use a flowchart

Flowcharts are great for giving directions because they show what to do step-by-step. They can also explain how things work or why things happen.

Read this passage about telephone calls. Use the information to fill in the flowchart on the left.

Phone Calls

A phone call begins when you punch the numbers on the keypad. This action creates an electric signal that is carried through thin cables to a central phone switch. The switch sends your call on its way using the numbers you punched as routing instructions. Next the signal goes to another switch and your call is sent to the number you are calling. Finally digital switches turn your voice into electrical impulses and carry it over the wires.

28
Copyright © 2002 LinguiSystems, Inc.

Strategic Learning
Reading Comprehension: Level 2

Sequencing

Goal: Use timelines and flowcharts to show sequencing

Circle the time words in this mixed-up story about rock 'n' roll history. Then put these events in chronological order in a timeline on another sheet of paper.

In the late 60s over 300,000 people attended a huge rock concert called Woodstock. Today rock music is the music of the world. MTV began to show rock music videos in 1981. In 1956 Elvis Presley became a superstar when he recorded "Heartbreak Hotel." Live Aid, an all-day rock concert to raise money for starving people in Africa, was held in July, 1985. "Rock Around the Clock" by Bill Haley and the Comets was the first rock 'n' roll hit in the early 1950s. The Beatles exploded onto the rock scene in 1962. Disco music and punk rock were the rage in the 1970s.

Read this story about the youngest U.S. president, John F. Kennedy. Draw a timeline and a flowchart on a sheet of paper. Record the events and dates on the timeline and how Kennedy became a hero on the flowchart.

JFK Becomes a Hero

After the attack on Pearl Harbor on December 7, 1941, John Fitzgerald Kennedy applied for sea duty in the United States Navy. Late in 1942, he was assigned to a PT boat squadron and soon became commander of PT Boat 109. On August 2, 1943, he and his squadron were patrolling in the South Pacific. The PT boat was cut in half by a Japanese destroyer. Two crewmen were killed; the other ten men clung to the wrecked boat for the rest of the night. Kennedy's back was injured. The next morning, Kennedy pulled one crewman safely to shore. Kennedy spent the next four days searching for help. On the fifth day, he found some friendly natives and convinced them to go for help. Kennedy and his crew were rescued on August 7, 1943. Kennedy was awarded the Navy and Marine Corps Medal for heroism and leadership and the Purple Heart for being wounded in combat.

Strategic Learning
Reading Comprehension: Level 2

Sequencing

> Goal: Use a timeline or flowchart to sequence events

Read this story about Stevie Wonder. Then make a timeline or a flowchart to show these events on another sheet of paper.

Stevie Wonder was born in 1950. Blind from birth, he displayed exceptional musical talent early in his life. Even as a toddler, he sang well and on key. He mastered the harmonica and drums at age seven. He then moved on to keyboards. He recorded his first hit, "Fingertips," in 1963 at the age of 13. Over the years, Stevie Wonder became an expert with synthesizers and other instruments. He became practically a one-man band in the recording studio. During the 60s, Wonder often hit the top charts with his own records and the songs he wrote for other musicians.

In 1971 Wonder's record contract with Motown expired. Wonder was free to do things his own way. He produced two hit albums. Over the next 11 years, he made seven more hit albums. His music showed the world his opinions on social issues.

Wonder has earned 17 Grammy Awards. He also won an Oscar for "I Just Called To Say I Love You" from the 1984 film *The Woman in Red*. Today he has had as many of his songs in the Top Ten as the Beatles and Elvis Presley ever did.

Wonder has sold more than 70 million LPs and ranks alongside the Beatles and Elvis Presley in having the most Top-Ten records. He is a remarkable American.

Sequencing

Goal: Understand spatial sequencing

Spatial sequencing is putting things in order from top to bottom, side-to-side, front-to-back, or in size order. When an object is described in a spatial sequence, you get a good mental picture of how it looks without seeing the object or a real picture of it.

Read this description of an insect. Then circle the types of spatial sequencing the author used to give you a mental picture of the insect. What insect do you think it is?

> This beautiful, delicate-looking insect has two pairs of large wings. The wings are covered with colorful, iridescent scales that overlap each other in perfectly formed rows. Sometimes this insect is so colorful, it is mistaken for a flower! Its body is divided into three sections: the head, the thorax, and the abdomen. The head has two antenna and two eyes. There are six legs attached to the thorax. The wings are attached to the middle section or thorax. The insect's body is covered by tiny sensory hairs.

1. This insect is a _____.

2. Circle the types of spatial sequencing used to describe the insect.

    top-to-bottom   side-to-side   front-to-back

3. Use spatial sequencing to describe something you see in your classroom. Then see if a partner can read your description and know what you have described.

_____
_____
_____
_____
_____
_____
_____
_____

Sequencing

> Goal: Use spatial sequencing

1. Read the descriptive statements about this famous statue.

    There is a torch in her right hand.

    She wears a seven-pointed crown on her head.

    A flowing robe covers her from shoulder to ankles.

    She has a book in her left hand.

    There are broken chains around her feet.

    She stands on a tall pedestal in the middle of an island.

    What is the name of this statue? _____

2. Use spatial sequencing to write an organized description of this sandwich.

    _____
    _____
    _____
    _____
    _____

    _____
    _____
    _____
    _____

Context Clues

Instructor Information

Goal: to use clues in pictures and text to figure out the meanings of unfamiliar words

Objectives: In this unit, your students will:

- identify and understand context clues
- use clues from pictures and words to understand what they read

Context clues are clues in pictures, words, and sentences that help students find out what words mean. When students don't know what a word means or are unfamiliar with a phrase, context clues can help them figure it out. Finding and using context clues requires students to evaluate and synthesize information to help them understand what they read.

In this unit, students will learn what context clues are. Students will use pictures, words, and sentences to help them identify and understand unfamiliar words they encounter in what they read.

Enrichment Activities

1. Hand out copies of the Context Clues Chart on page 36. Have your students use this chart to list new words they encounter in a particular curricular area. Encourage them to record any clues from words or pictures that could help them figure out what the unfamiliar words mean. Have them double-check their answers in a dictionary or text glossary for accuracy and make any necessary changes on their charts. Remind students to use this list to study for chapter or unit tests.

2. Clip comic strips from the newspaper. Cover up or cut out any text. Have your students use picture context clues to write their own words to go with the comic strips.

3. Bring in copies of news articles from a local newspaper. Have your students highlight words or phrases that they don't know. Then have them use context clues to figure out the meanings of the unfamiliar words. Compare results as a class.

Context Clues, continued

Instructor Information

4. Read a poem or story with made-up words, like "Jabberwocky" by Lewis Carroll. Since the words are made-up, they won't be in the dictionary and your students will need to use context clues for understanding.

5. Have your students use the meanings for base words and any suffixes or prefixes to help them understand unfamiliar words they encounter. For extra support, post a chart of common suffixes and prefixes and their meanings.

6. Remind your students that the context clues can be anywhere around the unfamiliar word. Encourage them to look back, forward, and way ahead for context in understanding the word. In other words, they should reread the paragraph before and scan the paragraph ahead to figure out what an unfamiliar word in a passage means.

7. Have students learn about context clues by creating their own context clues in a writing passage. Write five or six vocabulary words from a short story you are reading in class. Have your students use the vocabulary words in their own versions of the story, but have them include context clues for the new vocabulary words so that a much younger child would understand and enjoy the story.

8. Ask your students to think about the main idea and details of a passage as well as what they already know about the topic to understand what unfamiliar words mean.

Context Clues

> Goal: use context clues to determine the meanings of unfamiliar words

You're reading along and you stumble across a word you don't know. What should you do? Use context clues!

 Think about the **main idea**. What might the unfamiliar word mean in that context?

 If there is a **picture**, see if it helps you understand the word.

 Use what you already know. Take the word apart. Is there anything familiar about the word? Do you recognize the base word? What does the prefix or suffix mean?

 Look all around the word. Look for explanations, examples, synonyms, or antonyms for the unfamiliar word.

Here is an example.

When it became evident that the troops were losing, they became **mutinous**, refusing to obey their commanding officer. Rather than follow his instructions to dig in and fight, the troops retreated quickly into the hills.

What does the word *mutinous* mean in this passage?

1. Ask yourself what the passage is about. *(a battle)*

2. Look at any picture for additional clues. *(commanding officer looks frustrated; troops are running away)*

3. What do you know about the word? *(comes from the word* mutiny *)*

4. Check the words and sentences before and after the word. *(refusing to obey; rather than follow his instructions)*

Strategic Learning
Reading Comprehension: Level 2

Context Clues

Goal: Create and maintain a log of unfamiliar words and context clues

Use this chart to help you figure out what unfamiliar words mean. Check your answers in the dictionary or glossary of your textbook. Keep this chart handy to help you study for the next unit or chapter test.

Context Clues Chart for _____
(subject)

Words	Context Clues	Meanings

Context Clues

Goal: Use context clues to understand multiple-meaning words

Some words have more than one meaning. Look at the words before and after the bold words to figure out which meaning is being used in each sentence. Circle the correct meaning.

1. "What **kind** of flower is that?" Marisa asked.
    a. sort or type of something
    b. nice

2. Jack needs new lenses for his **glasses**.
    a. what you wear to see better
    b. what you drink out of

3. An earthquake happens when a **fault** in the earth moves.
    a. a mistake
    b. a crack in the earth

4. The visitors to the zoo watched the snake **shed** its skin.
    a. get rid of or take off
    b. a small building to keep things in

5. The crowd went **wild** as the runner crossed the finish line.
    a. not tame
    b. crazy; very excited

6. Mr. Henkle had to **charge** the shirt because he didn't have enough cash.
    a. to run quickly at someone or something
    b. to use a credit card; to pay for it later

7. My dog always stretches out on the floor and **pants** when she comes in from her walk.
    a. breathes heavily
    b. an item of clothing

Strategic Learning
Reading Comprehension: Level 2

Context Clues

Goal: Use affixes to understand unfamiliar words

Read each sentence and pay special attention to the bold words. Then use the chart to check the meaning of the prefix or suffix of each bold word. Use that information to help you understand what the bold words mean. Write the meanings in the chart below.

Prefixes	Meanings
bi-	two
co-	with; together
de-	away; from; off; down
un-	not; the reverse of

Suffixes	Meanings
-tion	act; quality; state; condition
-fy	become; cause; make
-able	able; likely
-ly	in a certain way; to a certain degree

1. The **copilot** took over the controls while the pilot took a break.
2. Daniel was eager to get a job after his **graduation** from high school.
3. Next weekend the **Biannual** Bike Races are held in Newton.
4. Mr. Parker's **unpersuasive** opinions lost him the election.
5. Trent learned to **liquify** metals in his science class today.
6. After taking the ticket off the windshield of his car, Mr. Todd **irritably** slammed the door.
7. The jeweler didn't have the exact ring Tisha wanted, but she showed Tisha a ring that was **comparable** in value.
8. The oppressed subjects joined together and vowed to **dethrone** the king.

Words	Meanings
1. copilot	
2. graduation	
3. biannual	
4. unpersuasive	
5. liquify	
6. irritably	
7. comparable	
8. dethrone	

Context Clues

Goal: Identify context clues for target words

Read each sentence and pay special attention to the bold words. Then read each sentence again and underline the context clues that help you understand what the bold words mean. Don't forget to check out the pictures for extra help, too.

1. Beavers have big **incisors** to bite through bark and nibble on logs as they build their wooden underwater homes.

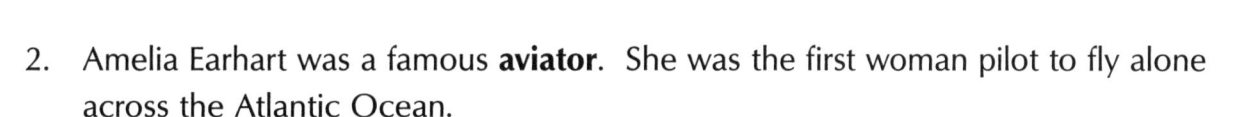

2. Amelia Earhart was a famous **aviator**. She was the first woman pilot to fly alone across the Atlantic Ocean.

3. The puffin is very unusual. It has a large, colorful bill and long feathers that **cascade** like a waterfall down the back of its head.

4. In science class, we're learning about **conifers**, which produce their seeds in cones, like pine trees.

5. A desert is so dry that only plants and animals that can **conserve** water are able to live there.

6. Sound cannot travel through a **vacuum**. There are no particles in the air to vibrate and pass the sound along.

7. Sometimes we find remains of living things that are **preserved** in rock. Scientists study these fossils to help us learn about our past.

Strategic Learning
Reading Comprehension: Level 2

39

Copyright © 2002 LinguiSystems, Inc.

Context Clues

Goal: Use context clues to understand unfamiliar words

Read each sentence and pay special attention to the bold words. Then read each sentence again and use the context clues to understand what the bold words mean. Write the meanings for these words in the chart below.

1. The hurricane winds gusted at incredible speeds, whipping trees from side to side. I couldn't believe the **velocity** of the winds!

2. Caesar made up a big fib about losing his homework. I can't believe he would **fabricate** such a story.

3. Montel carefully scraped the flaking paint off the old chair. He was happy with how the **restoration** was going.

4. Derrick sprayed more cleaner on the window. He rubbed and buffed until the window was **transparent** again.

5. Tracy bought shoes, jewelry, and other **accessories** to go with her new school clothes.

Words	Meanings
1. velocity	
2. fabricate	
3. restoration	
4. transparent	
5. accessories	

Context Clues

Goal: Use context clues to understand unfamiliar words

Read each sentence and pay special attention to the bold words. Then read each sentence again and use the context clues to understand what the bold words mean. Write the meanings in the blanks.

1. This was the most difficult assignment Miguel had ever seen. Every problem had him **baffled**.

    _____

2. The girls walked out of the movie theater where *Disgusting Killer* was playing. "That was **gruesome**," said Faith.

    _____

3. My grandfather has a lot of energy after he jogs. He is full of **vigor** for the rest of the day.

    _____

4. Mr. Reed heard two students shouting at each other. He ran to break up the **dispute**.

    _____

5. "Don't touch anything in my brother's room," said Shawn. "He's very **finicky** about his stuff."

    _____

Strategic Learning
Reading Comprehension: Level 2

Context Clues

Goal: Use context clues to understand unfamiliar words in a story

Read this passage. Then read it again. Use the context clues to figure out the meanings of the bold words and write the meanings below.

Sanford's favorite movie is *Space Creatures **Devour** New York City*. He especially loves the scene where the monsters eat the Empire State Building. The creatures all have transparent bodies, so you can see the huge bites of the **edifice** inside their stomachs. The buildings slowly **disintegrate** after they're eaten. When there's nothing left, the creature eats another one. The creatures are make-believe, of course, but they look very real. Sanford has always wondered how moviemakers create this **illusion**. He knows that one trick is to use **miniatures**. Special artists make these models for every scene.

1. devour   _____

2. edifice   _____

3. disintegrate   _____

4. illusion   _____

5. miniatures   _____

Context Clues

Goal: Use context clues to understand unfamiliar words in a passage

Read this passage. Then read it again. Use the context clues to figure out the meanings of the bold words and write the meanings below.

Shana was **ecstatic** about going out to her favorite restaurant, Italian Palace. She was really excited because she was celebrating her sixteenth birthday. Tonight the restaurant was having a buffet. Their buffet was known for its **abundance** of delicious **selections**. They had so many Italian dishes to choose from that it made her head spin just to think about it. The chef even made a special **concoction** just for Shana. It was an imaginative collection of rotini, ravioli, and linguini pasta with **marinara** sauce. This special tomato sauce was especially delicious. Shana was very impressed with the meal. She was stuffed, too!

1. ecstatic _____

2. abundance _____

3. selections _____

4. concoction _____

5. marinara _____

Strategic Learning
Reading Comprehension: Level 2

Context Clues

Goal: Use context clues to choose words to complete sentences

Use the context clues in each sentence to decide which word belongs in the blank.

| apathetic | digressed | quorum | optimistic | scaffold |
| cavalier | hoax | predicament | receptionist | utensils |

1. Tim found himself in a _____ when the battery died on his cell phone.

2. After the officer announced the bomb threat was a _____, the workers filed back into the office building.

3. When you have an _____ attitude, you try to think positively even in difficult situations.

4. Don't put large kitchen _____ like the spatula and the whisk in the dishwasher.

5. Darcy and her friends were so _____ that they didn't even want to participate in the school dance-a-thon.

6. When Evan's dad asked him about the car keys, Evan _____ by talking about the movie he saw last week.

7. Since there were only six members present, the council didn't have a _____ and couldn't vote on the issue.

8. With a _____ turn of her head, Kayla ignored the new girl's friendly greeting and walked right past her.

9. Watching the window washer working high above the ground on the _____ made me dizzy.

10. As Ian walked up to the window at his doctor's office, the _____ hung up the phone, looked up, and said, "Good morning. May I help you?"

Context Clues

Goal: Use context clues to select words to complete a story

Read this short story. Then read it again. Use the context clues in the story to choose the correct word from the box to write in each blank.

The _____ (1) from Franklin Middle School are excited today because they're taking a field trip to the courthouse. One of the students, Ramon, has a special reason for his _____ (2). His uncle is a judge and has agreed to _____ (3) them an interview.

The sixth grade students are very _____ (4) as they silently follow the guide into a courtroom. Judge Martinez is seated at a high desk and is wearing _____ (5) robes.

Sitting with his gavel in front of him, Judge Martinez _____ (6) the students' _____ (7). After the judge answers the final question, he announces that he has another _____ (8) and must leave. The students express their _____ (9) by giving him a round of applause.

fields
gratitude
enthusiasm
inquiries
judicial
pupils
grant
restrained
engagement

Strategic Learning
Reading Comprehension: Level 2

45
Copyright © 2002 LinguiSystems, Inc.

Context Clues

Goal: Use context clues to understand unfamiliar words in a story

Read this short story. Then read it again. Write any unfamiliar words in the chart below. Then use context clues from the passage to figure out what the words mean. Write the meanings in the chart.

Hawaii—A Tropical Paradise

When you think of Hawaii, you might envision a land with beautiful palm trees, surf, sand, sun, and fun. The many aquatic opportunities include surfing, boating, and swimming.

Hawaii offers more than just water activities. You can also visit a volcano to see where lava flows have left their mark. Geologists who study this hot, flowing rock ascertain many facts about volcanoes. Viewing these wonders gives you a look into the terrain of the islands.

Many exhilarating adventures await you in Hawaii. The climate is perfect for exciting outdoor activities that will take your breath away, like biking down the side of a volcano or parasailing high above the ocean. The food, the art, and the colorful clothing tell about the culture of the people who live there. A visit to Hawaii is truly a unique experience. Aloha!

Words	Meanings

Context Clues

Goal: Use context clues to understand unfamiliar words in a story

Read this story. Then read it again. Circle any unfamiliar words and look for context clues that help you understand their meanings. Then answer the questions at the bottom of the page.

There are also many theories about Earth as it is today. In the early 1900s, Alfred Wegener, a meteorologist, was interested in the study of weather. He was also interested in other sciences. In 1911 he claimed that Earth's continents were one huge body of land 200 million years ago. He named this landmass Pangaea. Wegener hypothesized, or suggested from scientific evidence, that Pangaea began to break apart about 180 million years ago. The pieces of land began to drift apart. These pieces are continents today. They are still drifting. At first scientists criticized his ideas. Today they accept his ideas because of convincing evidence.

Wegener gave several pieces of evidence for his theory. First, the continents fit together like a jigsaw puzzle. In fact, the continental shelves of South America are almost identical to those of Africa. Second, many similar rock layers across continents may have been one piece of land long ago. Third, evidence of glaciers has been found in South Africa. Fourth, fossil records show that similar plants and animals existed in what now are very different climates on continents far away from each other. Wegener's theory supports all these findings.

Use what you know from the story to answer these questions.

1. What would be the best title for this story?
   a. Old Fossils and Rock Layers
   b. A Crossword Puzzle
   c. Drifting Continents

2. What is **continental drift**?
   a. something that happens in a snowstorm
   b. a slow process in which pieces of a large chunk of land separate
   c. a theory about weather changes

3. What evidence supports Wegener's theory?
   a. Similar fossils exist in very different climates.
   b. Today's continents fit together like a jigsaw puzzle.
   c. Rock layers are similar across continents.
   d. a, b, and c

Predicting

> **Goal:** to use pictures and words to make predictions about stories and about characters' actions
>
> **Objectives:** In this unit, your students will:
>
> - predict the end of a story
> - predict what characters will think, do, or say
> - use prior knowledge and story clues to draw conclusions and make predictions
> - verify or revise predictions, based on new information

Making predictions about stories or about characters' actions requires students to evaluate information and make judgments about what they have read. Students need to know that picture and story clues can help them make predictions about what will happen next or what a character will say or do.

In this unit, students will predict what will happen next in a variety of reading passages. They will use prior knowledge and story clues to draw conclusions and to make predictions about stories and about characters. New information will give students an opportunity to change or check their predictions.

Enrichment Activities

1. Have your students watch a television show. During commercials, have them jot down what they think will happen next and why they think so. Then have them check their predictions as they continue to watch the show.

2. Bring a *TV Guide* to class. Read the title of one of the shows and have the students predict what it is about. Then read the summary about the show to check the accuracy of their predictions.

3. Group the students in pairs. Have one student in each pair write the beginning to a story. Next have the other student use predicting skills to write the next paragraph. Then have the first student write a paragraph, and so on, alternating until the story is completed.

Predicting, continued

4. During a story writing task, have your students write their stories without endings. Then have each student pass his paper to a partner. Have the partner read the story and, based on context clues from the story, write a predictable ending.

5. Choose a play your class is reading out loud. Stop at appropriate times throughout the play and ask students who are listening to predict what the next line will be. Continue reading to check their predictions.

6. Collect comic strips from newspapers. Cut off the last frame in each strip. Next have your students draw their own endings to the strips and share them with the class.

7. Teach your students to make predictions based on characters' feelings. Predicting about feelings helps some students learn how to predict events, since feelings are easily personalized.

8. Whenever students' predictions don't match what really happened, evaluate your students' use of clues and the extent of their background knowledge.

9. Help your students analyze the steps necessary for predicting, such as sequencing, making associations, and identifying the main idea and details.

10. Ask your students to make and record predictions about the content they encounter in topics they are studying. Have them verify or revise their predictions as they learn new information. This process should help them remember key information.

11. Before beginning a lesson, tell your students what you will teach. Ask them what they know about the topic. Then ask them to predict what they will learn. As you present the lesson, stop and have your students check their predictions, making modifications based on new information.

Predicting

Goal: use prior knowledge and story clues to draw conclusions and make predictions

As you read, you look for clues in a story to draw conclusions about people and events. You use these conclusions and what you already know to predict what might happen next. Use the following plan to make good predictions.

Clues + Conclusions + Knowledge = Predictions

See how this plan works with this story. Read the story first. Then look at the chart to see how the clues, conclusion, and knowledge guide you to make a good prediction.

> Melanie is shy. She doesn't like drawing attention to herself. The local animal shelter would like to present Melanie with an award for her efforts in raising money for the animals. Melanie will have to give a speech to accept the award. She is nervous, but she knows that the only way to conquer her fears is to face them.

Now that you have read this story, what do you predict will happen about Melanie? Look at the chart below.

Clues	+	Conclusions	+	Knowledge	=	Prediction
• Melanie is shy. • doesn't like attention drawn to herself		• Melanie is nervous about speaking to a group.		• The more you do something, the easier it gets.		• Melanie will succeed and become more confident giving speeches.

Predicting

Goal: Make predictions and change them, based on new information

Read the first sentence in each group. Think about the clues. Write your prediction on the line.

Then read the second sentence in each group and look for new clues. Write your new prediction on the next line.

1. Laura went to the hospital.

   Prediction _____

   She put on her uniform and reported to the nurses' station.

   Prediction _____

2. Joe ran as fast as he could.

   Prediction _____

   He heard the bell ring as he ran up the steps.

   Prediction _____

3. The boys sat still on the couch.

   Prediction _____

   Their mom put film in her camera.

   Prediction _____

4. Latasha opened the box.

   Prediction _____

   She had a bad cold.

   Prediction _____

5. Lynn signed her name on the form.

   Prediction _____

   The bank teller gave Lynn five dollars from her bank account.

   Prediction _____

Strategic Learning
Reading Comprehension: Level 2

Predicting

Goal: Draw conclusions to predict what will happen next

Read each passage and make a conclusion based on the clues in the story. Think about what you already know to predict what will happen next.

1. Aaron and Leo wanted tickets to see the rock group Vision. Tickets went on sale at 8:30 A.M. School started at 8:00. They skipped school and bought four tickets. As they were sneaking back into school, the principal caught them.

    a. What is your conclusion about what happened?

    _____

    b. What do you predict will happen?

    _____

2. Betsy hardly listened while her science teacher gave directions for the experiment. All of them seemed the same, anyway. Nothing exciting ever happened. Betsy looked over at the table of chemicals. She grinned and thought to herself, "Today will be different."

    a. What is your conclusion about what was happening?

    _____

    b. What do you predict will happen?

    _____

3. Andrew was late. His friends were at the door and were getting impatient. The movie started in five minutes and he couldn't find his wallet. He spotted his mom's purse on the table. There were two $5 bills in her wallet. "Oh, well, " Andrew thought as he grabbed the money. "Mom will never notice it's gone."

    a. What is your conclusion about happened?

    _____

    b. What do you predict will happen?

    _____

52

Copyright © 2002 LinguiSystems, Inc.

Strategic Learning
Reading Comprehension: Level 2

Predicting

Goal: Use context clues to make predictions

Read these stories. Draw a conclusion based on the clues in each story. Then think about what you already know and predict what will happen next.

1. Darren borrowed his brother's skateboard without asking. He took it to school and put it in his locker. When he returned later, the skateboard was gone.

    Conclusion _____

    Prediction _____

2. Alicia sat on the end of the bench. The black-and-white ball bounced out of bounds and she threw it back. She should have been the one scoring the point. Instead she was sitting with her leg propped up, watching her teammates win. Alicia thought about how the next game would be different.

    Conclusion _____

    Prediction _____

3. Tomorrow night was the Valentine's Day Dance. Anna thought Marcus was the secret admirer leaving those valentines in the locker she shared with her best friend, Tricia. Anna hoped Marcus would ask her to the dance. Just then, Anna saw Marcus walking with Tricia. Marcus was looking at Tricia, and Tricia was holding a pink carnation and smiling.

    Conclusion _____

    Prediction _____

Strategic Learning
Reading Comprehension: Level 2

Predicting

Goal: Use context clues to make predictions

Read these stories. Draw a conclusion based on the clues in each story. Then think about what you already know and predict what will happen next.

1. As Erik took his position on the field, he looked at the scoreboard. Only 39 seconds left in the game. It was fourth down and his team was behind by six points. This would be their last play unless they could get a first down. "Hut, hut, hut," yelled the quarterback. Erik started to run downfield. He turned just in time to see the ball sail over his head and hit the ground behind him.

   Conclusion _____

   Prediction _____

2. Kelly wrote the note quickly. She just HAD to tell her friend about the new hunk in her music class. Unfortunately, Kelly was so busy writing, she didn't notice her teacher moving slowly down the aisle toward her desk. Kelly froze as she heard a deep voice boom, "What do you have there, Ms. Malone?"

   Conclusion _____

   Prediction _____

3. Thea looked at the pile of unfinished homework on her desk. "I don't feel like doing this," she thought. "I'd rather watch TV and call some of my friends. I'll just pull double-duty tomorrow night." When she walked into math class the next day, she stopped dead in her tracks. Ms. Huxtable was putting paper and pens on all the desks.

   "Good morning, Thea," said Ms. Huxtable. "I hope you studied your lesson last night."

   Conclusion _____

   Prediction _____

Predicting

Goal: Use context clues to make predictions

Read each story. Predict what each character will say or do. Then read the ending of the story. See if your prediction was correct.

1. Mr. Hailey was sitting at his desk, grading papers. Two of his students, Jesse and A.J., came to the door. They asked him to play ball with them.

   What will Mr. Hailey say? _____

   _____

   Mr. Hailey looked at his watch. He said, "It would be fun to play with you. I have a lot of work to do, but I can play for 20 minutes. Okay?"

   A.J. smiled and threw Mr. Hailey the football.

   Was your prediction right? _____

   If your prediction wasn't right, how was it different from what happened? _____

   _____

2. Ellen looked at the mess in her room. Her mom told her she had to clean it before she could watch TV. Ellen's favorite program was on in ten minutes.

   What do you think Ellen will do? _____

   Ellen wanted to watch TV, so she worked as fast as she could. She hung up her clothes, made her bed, and put her books on the shelf. Ellen's room was clean in just 15 minutes!

   She only missed five minutes of her favorite show and she had a clean room.

   Was your prediction right? _____

   If your prediction wasn't right, how was it different from what happened? _____

   _____

Strategic Learning
Reading Comprehension: Level 2

Predicting

Goal: Make predictions and change them, based on new information

Read this story and make predictions about what will happen.

> **Small Sting**
>
> Karla concentrated on keeping still. "Don't move!" she told herself over and over. "I hope she doesn't use a long needle!" she thought.
>
> A woman in a white coat leaned close to her. "Now just relax. This will only sting a little," said the woman.

1. Predict what the woman in the white coat is going to do.

   _____

> The woman leaned closer. Karla held her breath. Suddenly she heard a loud SNAP! Karla jumped. Her heart was racing.
>
> "One more time," said the woman in the white coat. Karla heard another loud snap. "All done!" the woman said with a smile.

2. Predict what Karla is thinking now.

   _____

> Karla was surprised. It had stung a little, but it hadn't hurt that much.
>
> The woman in the white coat handed Karla a mirror. Karla smiled as she looked at her newly pierced ears.

3. Predict what Karla will say.

   _____

> "They look great!" said Karla. "I can't wait to show my friends!"

4. Were your predictions right? If not, how were your predictions different?

   _____

   _____

Predicting

Goal: Make predictions and change them, based on new information

Read this story and make predictions. As you learn more, change your predictions to fit the new information.

An Unlikely Hero

1. From the title, what do you think the story will be about?

___

> Molly Pitcher was born as Mary Ludwig on October 13, 1754. Her parents came from Germany and settled in New Jersey. When she grew up, Molly married John Casper Hays. Then the Revolutionary War began.

2. What do you think happened next?

___

> Molly's husband was a Continental soldier, so he joined the war. Molly wanted to help the cause, too.

3. What do you think happened next?

___

> Molly joined her husband on the battlefield. It was very hot. She carried pitchers of water to thirsty soldiers to drink and to cool off the cannons. That's how she got her nickname, "Molly Pitcher."

4. Was your last prediction correct? If not, explain how it was different.

___

> Molly also tended wounded men. During the battle at Monmouth, her husband fell from heatstroke.

5. What do you think happened next?

___

> Molly took her husband's place and fired his cannon at the British. She was the second woman to fire a cannon on an American battlefield.

6. Was your last prediction correct? If not, explain how it was different.

___

Predicting

> Goal: Draw conclusions to predict what will happen next

Read each story. Make a conclusion based on the clues you find. Then use what you already know to predict what will happen next.

1. Tasha walked out of the rest room. Rick stood along the row of lockers, surrounded by his friends. It was time to ask him to the dance. Tasha stood up straight and smiled broadly. "Hi, Rick! What's up?" she asked as she approached him. Suddenly Tasha felt her skirt. It was bunched up in the back and tucked into her pantyhose.

    Conclusion _____

    Prediction _____

2. The hair stylist stood in front of the mirror. "Almost done!" he said. He ran a comb through Cindy's hair and stepped back. Then his expression changed. "Um, since you've been so patient, uh, I won't charge you for this haircut," he said. He whirled Cindy's chair around and pushed her toward the door. As she passed by, Cindy heard a woman under a hair dryer gasp.

    Conclusion _____

    Prediction _____

3. "Arrggh!" groaned Kim as she wiped fingerpaint off her shoe. "You guys are driving me nuts!" she told the twins.

    The phone rang. It was Eric. "Hey, turn on the TV to Channel 6. *Hit Parade* is showing the Stingers' new video."

    Kim glanced at the twins busily fingerpainting at the table. "You guys just keep playing nicely, okay?"

    Conclusion _____

    Prediction _____

Predicting

Goal: Predict what characters will think, do, or say

Read this story and make predictions about what will happen.

The April evening was cool and breezy. Josh pulled his jacket closer as he ran down his street. When he reached his house, he ran up the back stairs and guiltily slunk in the back door. His family was already eating dinner.

"You're late. Where have you been?" asked his stepmom.

Josh looked at the floor and tried to look guilty. "Just, uh, out with the guys. Sorry I'm late." He sat down at his place at the table, leaving his jacket on.

"Josh, why don't you take off your jacket?" asked his sister.

"Why don't you mind your own business?" snapped Josh.

His stepmom gave him a puzzled look. Josh suppressed a grin.

1. What is Josh's stepmom thinking?

   _____

The meal went on. Finally Josh's dad said, "Josh, it's warm in here. You're sweating. Are you sick? Why don't you take your jacket off?"

"I'm fine!" snapped Josh, as he pulled off his jacket. His family gasped as they saw a tattoo of a snake on his arm.

2. What will Josh's family say?

   _____

"Joshua Gomez, what have you done?" said his dad. His stepmom gasped. His sister just laughed. She loved it when Josh got in trouble.

3. What will Josh do?

   _____

"Relax!" Josh said with a smile. "It's just a temporary tattoo!"

4. Were your predictions right? If not, how were they different?

   _____

Strategic Learning
Reading Comprehension: Level 2

Predicting

> Goal: Predict what characters will think, do, or say

Read this story and make predictions about what will happen.

Wade couldn't believe it. Usually he warmed the bench, but tonight the coach was sending him in to play. He took off his warm-up jacket and joined the huddle.

1. Predict what Wade is thinking. _____

   The huddle broke and Wade ran out on the floor. The gym vibrated with cheers and the band played the school song. Wade took a deep breath and thought, "I hope I don't mess up my big chance!" The referee blew his whistle and play started. The tipped ball went to Wade.

2. Predict what Wade will do. _____

   Wade dribbled quickly down the floor. No one was around him except his teammate Andrew. Wade thought he heard Andrew call to him to pass him the ball, but Wade was wide open for a lay-up and he took it. Perfect! The ball swished through the net. Wade turned excitedly toward Andrew.

3. Predict what Andrew will say. _____

   "Nice going, Wade," said Andrew. "You just scored two points for the other team."

4. Predict what Wade will do. _____

   Wade looked around at the crowd, which was very quiet. He walked briskly off the court and into the locker room. When the game ended, Wade told the team, "Hey, guys, I'm really sorry about what happened." Andrew grabbed Wade's shoulder.

5. Predict what Andrew will say. _____

   "That's okay, Wade," smiled Andrew. "Anyone can make a mistake. But from now on, you have a new nickname. You are Wrong-Way Wade!"

6. Were your predictions right? If not, how were they different?

   _____

Predicting

Goal: Use context clues in passages to make predictions

Look for clues in these stories to predict what will happen next. Then write your predictions.

The phone rang and rang, but no one answered. "He must be on his way," thought Alice. She hung up the pay phone and walked back to her booth.

The waiter again asked Alice if she'd like to order. "No, I told you, I'm waiting for someone," Alice said. She wished the waiter would chill out. He'd asked for her order twice already. After all, Raj was only 30 minutes late.

1. Prediction _____

Pepe's economics class was selling pretzels for a group ski trip. Pepe was sick of trying to juggle his books and a huge bag of pretzels all around school. "I'll just leave it in here during fifth period," he thought as he set the pretzels in his locker. When he returned later, the pretzels were gone.

2. Prediction _____

Tom strutted into the restaurant and found Maria, the manager. "Hi. I'm here about the dishwashing job," he said. Maria motioned for him to sit in a nearby booth. Tom leaned back in his seat and put his feet up. Maria began to speak, but Tom interrupted her. "I don't work weekends or before 10 in the morning. I don't like people bossing me around, either," Tom explained. He grinned at Maria and waited for her to speak.

3. Prediction _____

Sara finished painting the Homecoming Dance poster and leaned it against the wall to dry. She felt a little low. She was in charge of decorating, but she didn't have a date for the dance. "Hi, Sara. The, uh, posters look really, um, nice," said a shy voice behind her. It was George.

"Hi, George," Sara said absentmindedly. George cracked his knuckles nervously and looked at the floor. He cleared his throat.

4. Prediction _____

Strategic Learning
Reading Comprehension: Level 2

Cause and Effect

Instructor Information

Goal: to understand and explain relationships between causes (reasons) and effects (results)

Objectives: In this unit, your students will:

- identify causes and effects in sentences and stories
- understand multiple causes and effects
- use signal words to identify causes and effects
- identify possible causes
- identify positive and negative effects
- apply knowledge of cause and effect to make decisions

Understanding cause and effect requires students to use logical thinking skills as they evaluate information and make judgments based on what they have read. They need to understand that for every cause, or reason, there is an effect, or result.

In this unit, students will identify causes and effects in a variety of ways. Signal words will help them identify the causes and effects in different reading passages. Once students can successfully identify causes and effects, they will use what they have learned to make decisions.

Enrichment Activities

1. Ask your students to make a list of three things that happened yesterday or today at school or at home. Then have them draw diagrams like the one below to list the causes and effects. (Copy the diagram on the board as a model.) If there is more than one cause, have them add more ovals and connect them to the effect box.

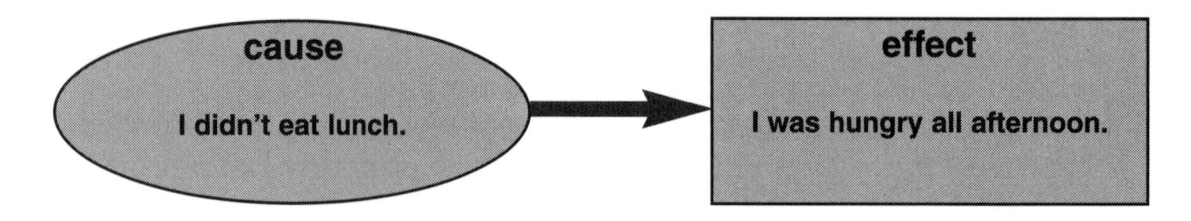

cause
I didn't eat lunch. → **effect** I was hungry all afternoon.

Cause and Effect, continued

Instructor Information

2. Give your students effects that have several possible causes, such as detention. Have students think of as many causes as they can within a certain time limit. Extend this activity by asking students to listen to national news and having them identify causes and effects in what they hear. Then decide as a group if there could have been other causes for each effect.

3. Help students understand that one cause can have multiple effects, such as a thunderstorm causing flooding, fires, and dangerous driving conditions. One effect can also be caused by several things. For example, feeling tired can be caused by a combination of strenuous physical activity, lack of sleep, and a poor diet.

4. Science experiments are full of causes and effects. Here's a quick, easy experiment. You'll need an empty soda can, a blown-up balloon, and your hair.

   Put the can on its side on a table or the floor. Make sure the can isn't moving. Rub the balloon back and forth quickly on your hair. Hold the balloon about one inch in front of the can. Then have students draw, write, or talk about what you did (the cause) and what happened (the effect).

   Next turn on a faucet and let the water run lightly. Rub the balloon on your hair again and hold the balloon near the water. Have students draw, write, or talk about what you did (the cause) and what happened (the effect).

5. Ask your students, "What school rule would you like to change?" Then have students state rules and tell how they'd like to change them. Have them identify both positive and negative effects of such changes in the school rules.

6. Ask students to identify causes and effects as they read in class, try to solve problems with peers, and when they're affected by situations in their communities or at school.

7. Whenever your students seem to be convinced that there is only one possible cause for a given effect, help them brainstorm multiple causes.

Cause and Effect

Goal: understand that a cause (or reason) has a effect (or result)

A **cause** is WHY something happened. An **effect** is WHAT happened.

        Cause   Effect
You studied hard, so you got an A on your test.

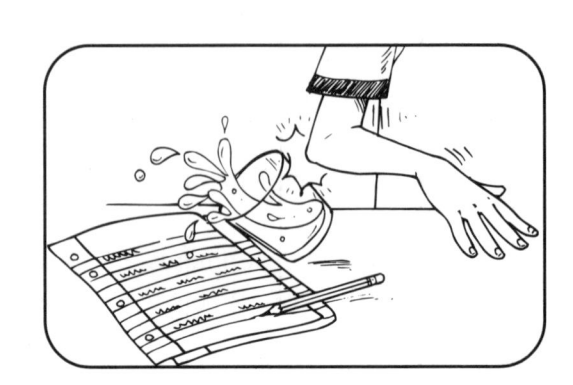

This plan will help you find causes and effects in reading.

✦ Ask yourself, "What happened?" The answer is the **effect**. The effect is underlined in these sentences.

    Jake bumped the table and <u>the water spilled</u>.

    Because the water spilled, <u>Jake's homework was ruined</u>.

✦ Ask yourself, "Why did it happen?" The answer is the **cause**. The cause is underlined in these sentences.

    <u>Jake bumped the table</u> and the water spilled.

    <u>Because the water spilled</u>, Jake's homework was ruined.

Hint: When you see a signal word, you'll probably find a cause and effect nearby. Look for these signal words.

because	so	therefore	since
in order to	as a result	the reason	

Remember, an effect can have more than one cause and a cause can have more than one effect.

Cause and Effect

Goal: Identify possible causes

Circle the letters of the causes that make sense for each item. Then add one or two more ideas.

1. Why might a person become a teacher?
   a. to help others
   b. because teaching is fun
   c. to be like a teacher the person admired

   _____

   _____

2. Why might a person become a volunteer?
   a. to make money
   b. to gain experience in a work situation
   c. to meet new people

   _____

   _____

3. What might cause someone to join a club?
   a. to have fun
   b. to learn new skills
   c. to meet new people

   _____

   _____

4. Why might a person write a letter to a newspaper?
   a. to share strong feelings about something
   b. to share personal opinions with others
   c. to see his/her name in print

   _____

   _____

5. Why would a person become a vegetarian?
   a. because gardening is fun
   b. to protect animals
   c. to eat a healthier diet

   _____

   _____

6. Why might a person become a doctor?
   a. to work long hours
   b. to help others
   c. interested in medicine/science

   _____

   _____

7. What might cause someone to get a job?
   a. wants/needs the money
   b. to get out of the house
   c. to learn new skills

   _____

   _____

8. Why would a person start an exercise program?
   a. to be healthy/strong
   b. to lose weight
   c. to have fun

   _____

   _____

Strategic Learning
Reading Comprehension: Level 2

Cause and Effect

Goal: Identify possible effects

Check the effects that make the most sense. Then think of one or two of your own ideas.

1. A tornado has very high winds. The winds form a cloud shaped like a funnel. This cloud is like a giant vacuum cleaner. What are some effects of a tornado?
   ___ buildings destroyed   ___ flooding   ___ trees pulled out

2. When warm, humid air rises, a thunderstorm can happen. The air forms a cloud. Then the air races around inside the cloud. This creates electricity, also known as lightning. What are some effects of a thunderstorm?
   ___ power goes out   ___ wind damage   ___ a snowstorm

3. When temperatures drop below freezing, it can snow. Snow and wind together causes a snowstorm. What are some effects of a snowstorm?
   ___ a thunderstorm   ___ freezing cold   ___ hazardous driving conditions

4. A hurricane forms over water. Very high winds with a thunderstorm can cause a hurricane. It can last for several days. What are some effects of a hurricane?
   ___ flooding   ___ a volcano erupts   ___ buildings destroyed

5. A flood occurs when there is too much water and no place for it to go. The extra water can come from a huge amount of rain and/or ice melting on a river. What are some of the effects of a flood?
   ___ farmland ruined   ___ people homeless   ___ damage from high winds

6. A volcano forms when the pressure under the ground gets too great. Molten rock (lava) and steam erupt. They shoot high into the sky. As the lava cools, it turns to ash and falls on the ground. What are some effects of a volcano erupting?
   ___ people homeless   ___ freezing cold   ___ wildlife killed

7. Droughts happen when there is no rain for a long period of time. Rivers dry up. Land gets dried out. What are some effects of a drought?
   ___ power goes out   ___ crops can't grow   ___ increased risk of wildfires

8. An ice storm covers everything in ice. What are some effects of an ice storm?
   ___ hazardous driving   ___ buildings destroyed   ___ power out

Cause and Effect

Goal: Identify positive and negative effects

Some causes can have both positive and negative effects. Here's an example.

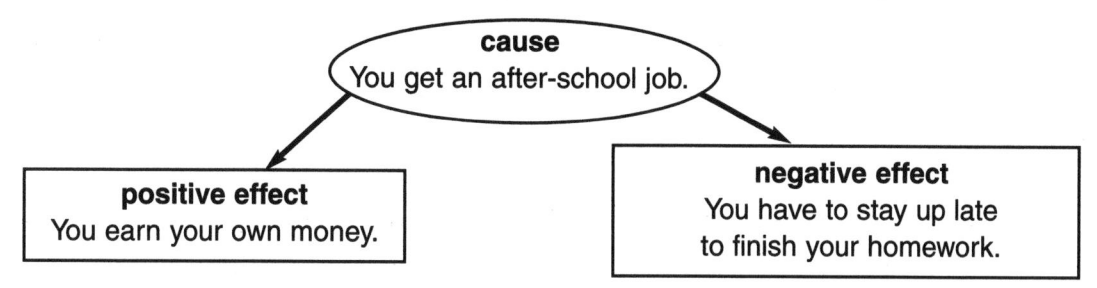

cause
You get an after-school job.

positive effect
You earn your own money.

negative effect
You have to stay up late to finish your homework.

Write at least one positive effect and one negative effect for each cause below.

1. You decide to redecorate your room.

   positive effect _____

   negative effect _____

2. You don't like the music your brother is listening to on the radio, so you change the station.

   positive effect _____

   negative effect _____

3. You hang out with friends instead of helping your grandmother clean her basement.

   positive effect _____

   negative effect _____

4. You get a parakeet.

   positive effect _____

   negative effect _____

5. You stay up all night at a friend's house.

   positive effect _____

   negative effect _____

Strategic Learning
Reading Comprehension: Level 2

Cause and Effect

Goal: Identify causes and effects

Underline the effect in each sentence and circle the cause. Remember to ask yourself these questions.

What happened? (the effect)   **Why did it happen?** (the cause)

1. I have to move to the basement because my grandfather is coming to live with us.

2. Because our teacher was sick, the math test was postponed until Monday.

3. Grace's mom got called into work, so Grace had to baby-sit.

4. Blake has a broken leg because he was showing off on his skateboard.

5. Since so many people wanted to buy tickets, two more shows were added.

6. We were late for the concert, so we didn't have any dinner.

7. There was a huge snowstorm, so we stayed an extra day.

8. Kate and Kelly stayed up late since there was no school tomorrow.

9. My shoes stuck to the floor because someone had spilled juice on it.

10. Owen ate ten brownies, and as a result, he had a terrible stomachache.

Cause and Effect

Goal: Identify a series of causes and effects

Often one event causes a second event that causes a third event, and so on. Read each story. Fill in the flowchart to show the series of causes and effects. The first one is started for you.

1. It should be against the law to burn leaves. When leaves are burned, smoke goes into the air, causing air pollution. Because of the pollution, many people have trouble breathing. Then they end up at the hospital with breathing problems.

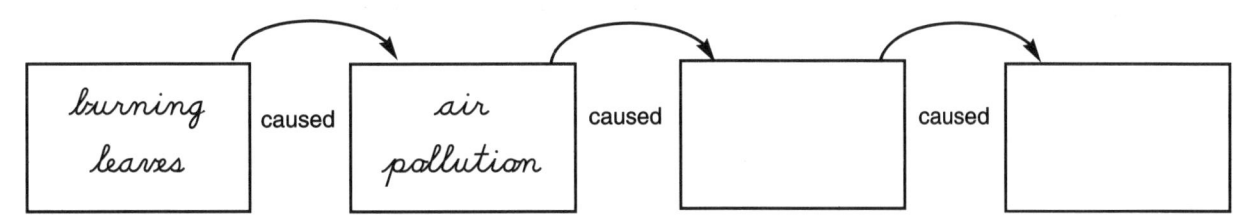

   [burning leaves] caused → [air pollution] caused → [ ] caused → [ ]

2. Dogs should not be allowed to run around loose. Some dogs are dangerous. They should not be outside without being on a leash. As a result of dogs roaming free, many people get attacked by dogs each year. Because of this danger, dog owners should be required to keep their dogs on leashes.

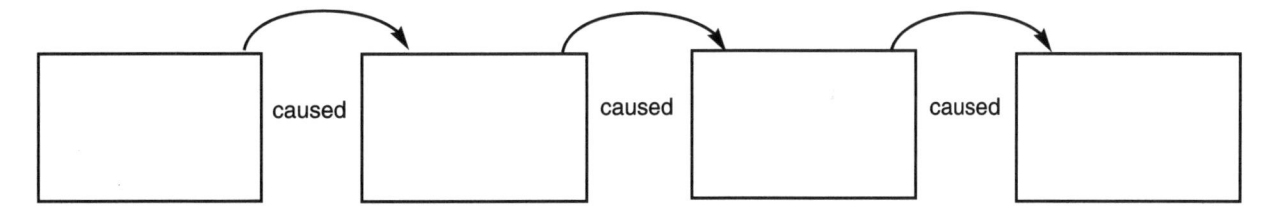

   [ ] caused → [ ] caused → [ ] caused → [ ]

3. Oil spills cause lots of problems. Many birds and animals die. Much money and time have to go into the cleanup. Some people even lose their jobs. For example, if an oil spill happens where fishermen catch fish to sell, an oil spill can kill the fish they need to catch.

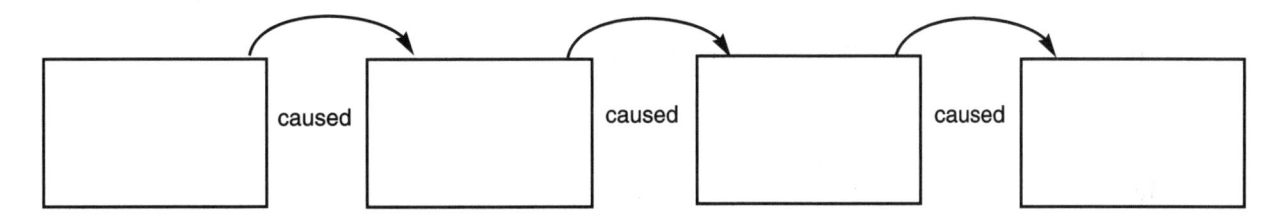

   [ ] caused → [ ] caused → [ ] caused → [ ]

Cause and Effect

> Goal: Answer cause and effect questions about paragraphs

Read these stories and answer the questions.

Dawn held her breath as her teacher handed back the reports. Dawn had rushed through her report, so she was anxious to see how she did. Mrs. Royce smiled at Dawn as she handed her the report. When Dawn opened the cover, she let out a sigh of relief. She had gotten 45 out of 50 points!

1. What was the cause of Dawn's anxiety?

   _____

The basketball team sat quietly on the bus. No one was cheering. They had lost the last game of the season. Then the coach started talking. He talked about how proud he was of the players. He congratulated the players on playing a good game, even though they lost. By the time they got back to school, the players felt much better. They let out one big cheer before getting off the bus.

2. Why was the basketball team so quiet on the bus?

   _____

3. Why did the coach talk to the players?

   _____

Max and Abby went to their swimming lesson. When Max got out of the pool, he ran to get his towel. Then he slipped and fell. Their teacher was glad Max was okay, but he was kind of mad, too, because he had told both of them not to run around the pool. Before Max and Abby went home, they reviewed the pool rules again.

4. What caused Max to slip and fall?

   _____

5. What might be two effects of not following pool rules?

   _____

   _____

Cause and Effect

Goal: Answer cause and effect questions

Answer each question.

1. Why should people wear bike helmets when riding bikes, skateboards, or scooters?
   _____

2. Why should children eat healthy foods?
   _____

3. What is one reason students should keep their lockers clean?
   _____

4. Why should children get lots of sleep?
   _____

5. What is one reason a student might not turn in his or her homework?
   _____

6. What is one positive effect of doing homework?
   _____

7. What is one negative effect of getting a new puppy?
   _____

8. What is one positive effect of smiling at people?
   _____

9. What is one negative effect of not eating breakfast?
   _____

10. Write two effects of getting up really early.
    _____
    _____

Strategic Learning
Reading Comprehension: Level 2

Referents

> **Goal:** to understand that pictures or words can represent other words
>
> **Objectives:** In this unit, your students will:
> - understand that words or phrases can substitute for referents
> - identify referents in sentences
> - add referents in order to complete sentences
> - identify referents described by participial or gerund phrases
> - identify referents in a variety of reading passages

Instructor Information

For reading success, students must be able to identify and understand words that refer to or substitute for other words. Students must be able to make the connection between these words or phrases to comprehend what they are reading.

In this unit, students will first understand that pictures and symbols can take the place of words. Then they will learn about common word substitutions and identify the referents for words or phrases in sentences and stories.

Enrichment Activities

1. Take your students on a walk around the school. Talk about the signs and symbols you see. Have students tell you what each one stands for. For example, point out the flag that represents our country and freedom. Use these words and phrases in your discussion: *means*, *stands for*, *substitutes for*, and *represents*.

    After your walk, make a list on the board of some of the signs and symbols you saw. Ask students to review what each one stands for.

2. Have students write autobiographies using the word *I* and other words or phrases that refer to themselves. First have them list words or phrases that talk about themselves. Then have them put the words and phrases into sentences and write paragraphs about themselves. When they're done, have them make a list of each word or phrase

Referents, *continued*

> Instructor Information

that refers to a referent, including all the ways they refer to themselves. Here's an example:

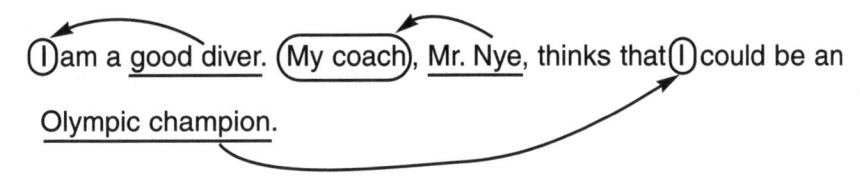

(I) am a good diver. (My coach), Mr. Nye, thinks that (I) could be an Olympic champion.

3. Have students find word referents in stories they are currently reading. You can have them look at each page or each chapter, depending on the book. List the word referents they find on the board. Talk about what each word or phrase refers to (the referent).

4. Write your name on the board. Then write as many ways to refer to yourself as you can think of. Review them with your students and explain that each description refers to you. Next give each student an index card. Ask students to write their names on one side and all the ways they can think of to refer to themselves on the other side. Have students volunteer to share the information on their cards.

5. Write a sentence on the board. Ask several students to rewrite it and substitute words or phrases that refer to the original people, places, or things in your sentence.

6. Let your students draw or make a bulletin board of someone they are studying or someone famous. Around the picture, position words or phrases that refer to that person.

7. If a student uses pronouns in conversation without stating their referents, ask him questions to help him clarify what he is saying. Talk about the need to state specific nouns before you refer to them with pronouns. Nouns are "teachers" and pronouns are "substitutes."

8. Have your students talk about someone they all know. Brainstorm a list of referents for that person on the board.

9. Play a version of *Trivial Pursuit*. Write character descriptions from stories or about people in your school on slips of paper. Also write the name of the character, the referent. Divide the class into teams. One team member reads a character description to the other team and the team guesses the character's name. (Set a time limit of one or two minutes per character.) Teams then switch roles. The team that identifies the most characters in a specified time limit wins.

Referents

Goal: understand referents

What happens when your teacher is sick? Right, you have a substitute teacher. The substitute takes the place of your regular teacher.

Words can have substitutes, too. The words they substitute for are called **referents**. The substitute words or phrases refer to the referents.

(Laura) loves to read. In fact, <u>this bookworm</u> reads for an hour every morning and for an hour every night!

    The referent here is *Laura*. The phrase *this bookworm* refers back to Laura.

(Rick) was sleepy. <u>He</u> could hardly stay awake in class.

    The referent here is *Rick*. The pronoun *he* refers back to Rick.

Here's a plan to help you understand referents.

◆ Look for a word or phrase that might substitute for another word. Underline it.

    Grandpa taught me how to play gin rummy. I love to play that <u>card game</u>.

◆ Ask yourself **who**, **what**, or **where** the word or phrase is talking about. Circle the word and draw an arrow to it.

    Grandpa taught me how to play (gin rummy.) I love to play that <u>card game</u>.

◆ Check the meaning of the word or phrase substitute. Does the word referent mean almost the same thing as the word it replaces?

    Yes. Gin rummy is a card game.

Referents

Goal: Identify referents in sentences

Draw an arrow from the underlined word or words to the referent. Then circle the referent. The first one is done for you.

1. I'm going for a ride in our (automobile). I'll go get in the car now.

2. I love shooting hoops with my brother. Playing basketball is my favorite thing to do.

3. Grandma Jansen fixed salmon last night. The fish tasted great.

4. Keesha really liked her birthday present from James. It was the best gift she'd ever gotten.

5. Trey helps Sara with her history. Sara's tutor is very patient.

6. My stepmom bought some SportsStar shoes for me. My new tennis shoes are gray with white stripes.

7. I hate cleaning my room. This job takes so long to do!

8. Lucas and I love playing baseball in the vacant lot. Sometimes we have to share our favorite place with other kids.

9. My family is going to the school concert tonight. It will be a great show!

10. Our class needs a project to earn money for our class trip. Maybe we could try having a bake sale.

Now check your work. Say the words you circled in the place of the underlined word or words in the second sentence. Does the sentence mean almost the same thing?

Example: I'm going for a ride in our **automobile**. I'll go get in the **automobile** now.

Strategic Learning
Reading Comprehension: Level 2

Referents

Goal: Identify referents in sentences

Draw an arrow from the underlined word or words to its referent. Then circle the referent.

1. I take photographs of my friends. I save these pictures to laugh about later.

2. Earth is the third planet from the sun. This energy source provides heat and light to our planet.

3. It was time for exams at school. The tests made everyone nervous.

4. Jake is learning to speak Spanish. He has been studying the language for two years.

5. I often drink hot chocolate. I like the warm drink best with a little peppermint in it.

6. Suzanne Simon is a great actress. This movie star has been in over 50 films!

7. Is zero a number? This special symbol means nothing.

8. Ellen went to the market to buy groceries. She took the food home to make dinner.

9. Brett likes to look at star formations in the night sky. He is studying constellations at school.

10. It is warm in Florida almost all year. Many people travel to this state each year.

11. Shane washed his jeans with bleach. He thought that would make his pants look cool.

Referents

Goal: Use referents to complete sentences

Choose the correct referent from the box to complete each sentence.

> Abraham Lincoln   Rachel and Ellie
> dairy products   the Liberty Bell
> Atlantic Ocean   these instruments
>   Mark Twain

1. _____ are in my class. Those two girls look enough alike to be twins.

2. We watched a movie about the _____. That body of water is huge!

3. How are a piano and a guitar alike? _____ both have strings.

4. I like _____. In fact, I eat milk and cheese every day.

5. _____ wrote many great stories. That fine author had a way with words that delighted his readers.

6. _____ died in 1865. The 16th President of the United States is buried in Springfield, Illinois.

7. Have you ever seen _____? That freedom symbol is in Philadelphia.

Referents

Goal: Use referents to complete sentences

Choose the correct referent from the box to complete each sentence.

> Hawaii   Tanya
> art supplies   team sports
> beautiful flowers   wetlands
> Johnson Elementary School

1. _____ smell so good. Roses and carnations come in such pretty colors.

2. _____ is a beautiful state. Many people visit the islands every year.

3. I love _____. I try to play soccer and basketball every Saturday.

4. The PTA bought _____ for the first graders. These paints and crayons should be kept in the art closet.

5. _____ has the fewest students in the city. That old building is going to be closed next year.

6. _____ are places where the ground is soaked with water for at least part of the year. These swamps, marshes, and bogs are usually found near lakes, rivers, or oceans.

7. _____ swims with her swim team every day. This dedicated athlete plans to be an Olympic champion someday.

Referents

Goal: Identify referents in a passage

Find the referent for each underlined word and circle it. Then draw an arrow from the underlined word to its referent.

Joseph: You should have been on our bus this morning. Luke's birthday is today, and Kate and Maya gave him¹ a big surprise. It was very funny.

James: Haley was there. She² said that Kate and Maya always give Luke a hard time.

Joseph: Well, today the girls didn't say a word to him³. Luke was busy studying for a science test, so he⁴ didn't notice. Then Kate asked him if she⁵ could borrow his history book. When he reached under his seat to get it⁶, a big, hairy hand grabbed him. Boy, did he yell!

James: Kate and Maya must have borrowed the gorilla suit from the school play. Those girls⁷ are really silly!

◇ ◇

Anna: My dad rented the movie *Stranded* last night. It⁸ was about a boy who was left at home by mistake when his parents went on a trip. I thought the kid⁹ was pretty funny.

Amber: I've seen that movie. It was funny, but I think being left behind while your family is gone could be pretty scary. The burglars were really goofy guys¹⁰, weren't they? Josh was way smarter than they were!

Anna: Yeah, Josh was smart, especially when he¹¹ made his house look like it was full of people having a party. Remember what his family did when they¹² realized he wasn't with them? His mom flipped out! She¹³ went crazy.

Amber: I thought the burglar with the gold tooth was kind of cool. He wasn't too smart, but he was a neat guy¹⁴.

Strategic Learning
Reading Comprehension: Level 2

Referents

Goal: Identify referents in a passage

As you read the story below, find the referents for the underlined words. Circle each referent. Then draw an arrow from the underlined words to their referents.

I was the youngest of five children. Our home was a tiny place¹ with no indoor plumbing. My parents worked hard to provide our food and clothing. We never took a vacation.

Once I learned to read, life was not the same! I met Charles Dickens and he² led me through the streets of London. The people he introduced me to were folks with all kinds³ of backgrounds.

Mark Twain took me on trips down the Mississippi River. The raft built by Huckleberry Finn was my vessel⁴ as Mr. Twain painted pictures of the young boy's⁵ adventures with his storytelling.

The events I read about seemed real. Books were my time⁶ machine. Reading was my ticket⁷ around the world.

As an adult, I have visited some of the places I had read about. Nothing I have seen has shown me the world the way I first saw it⁸ in books.

80

Copyright © 2002 LinguiSystems, Inc.

Strategic Learning
Reading Comprehension: Level 2

Referents

Goal: Identify referents in a story

Read each story. When you are done, go back and underline all of the word substitutes that refer to Lance Armstrong, Michelle Kwan, and Mia Hamm.

1. Lance Armstrong is one of the best cyclists in the world. This world champion has won many bike races all over the world. He is most famous for winning the grueling Tour de France race three years in a row. He is a two-time Olympian. Lance is also a cancer survivor. He beat the odds and is stronger than ever. He has become a role model for all aspiring athletes.

2. Michelle Kwan is a great figure skater. She has skated her way right into the record books. This Queen of the Ice won five straight U.S. championships. She has been named Figure Skater of the Year five times. She has earned more perfect scores in competition than any other skater, male or female. Michelle has won two Olympic medals. This young woman has melted the hearts of her fans.

3. Mia Hamm is a great soccer player. In fact, she is one of the best in the world. She was the youngest player ever to play on the U.S. national team. She won the U.S. Soccer's Female Athlete of the Year award five times. She won a gold medal in the Olympics. The 5'5" forward has used her fame to set up the Mia Hamm Foundation. As spokesperson, one of her goals is to empower young female athletes. She is a great role model for young women.

Referents

Goal: Identify referents in a story

Read each story. Then follow the directions under each story.

1. Hachiko was Mr. T's dog. She followed him to the train station every day when he went to work. She met her master there every night when he came home.

   One evening Mr. T didn't get off the train. Hachiko waited for the man all night at the station. People tried to help her, but they couldn't make the poor dog feel better. She didn't understand that Mr. T had died.

   Hachiko went to the train station every night for ten years. People got to know her. They fed her. They took care of Mr. T's faithful companion.

   There is a statue of Hachiko today in the train station so everyone will remember her.

   Now underline all the words that refer to Hachiko. Circle the words that refer to Mr. T.

2. Max the mouse was minding his own business in a hotel room. Then the housekeeper came in with her vacuum. The little critter dashed under the bed. He hoped the strong machine wouldn't come near him. The busy worker vacuumed all around, but she didn't get to Max. That clever fellow was too far under the bed for the noisy monster to grab him. When the woman left, Max ran out from his hiding place. "Whew, what a close call!" he sighed with relief.

   Now underline all of the words that refer to Max. Circle the word referents that refer to the housekeeper. Then draw a box around the words that refer to the vacuum.

Referents

Goal: Identify referents in a story

Read each story. Then underline all of the words that refer to German shepherds and the Mississippi River.

1. Have you ever seen a German shepherd? Maybe you know someone who owns this type of dog. German shepherds are working dogs. These fine animals came from northern Europe many years ago. They have traveled far from their native land where they protected flocks of sheep.

    German shepherds are very brave. They have been used to help police officers catch criminals. In fact, these "police dogs" are so brave that soldiers use them as guard dogs.

    These gentle creatures are very smart and very loyal. That is why they make great Seeing-Eye dogs.

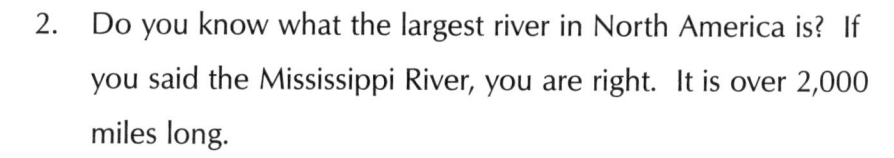

2. Do you know what the largest river in North America is? If you said the Mississippi River, you are right. It is over 2,000 miles long.

    Years ago, when the river was being mapped out, it was called a "gathering of waters." It was also called "Big River" or "Father of Waters." Whatever its name, it is one of the world's most famous rivers.

    This grand body of water has many uses. It is a home for fish and wildlife. It is used for boating and fishing. It is used to transport items on barges.

    Many people enjoy the beauty and history of this great waterway each year.

Strategic Learning
Reading Comprehension: Level 2

Referents

Goal: Identify referents and answer questions

Read each paragraph. Then think about referents to help you answer the questions.

1. Molly takes voice lessons because she likes to sing. She hopes to be a professional singer someday. Molly likes her voice coach. He thinks she has real talent.

    a. Who takes voice lessons? _____

    b. What does she want to be someday? _____

    c. Is Molly's voice coach a man or a woman? _____

2. Will helps Paul with his math problems twice a week. Paul needs a tutor to help him understand his homework.

    a. Who is the tutor? _____

    b. Who needs help with math? _____

    c. Why does he need a tutor? _____

3. Emma had a party for Steve. He was surprised because it was a week before his birthday.

    a. Who was the party for? _____

    b. Who gave him the party? _____

    c. What was a week before his birthday? _____

4. Mr. and Mrs. Keene drove Laura and Ellen to school before they headed to work. They dropped the girls off in front of the building.

    a. Who went to school? _____

    b. Who are "they"? _____

    c. What building were the girls dropped off in front of? _____

Referents

Goal: Identify referents and answer questions

Read each paragraph. Then think about referents to help you answer the questions.

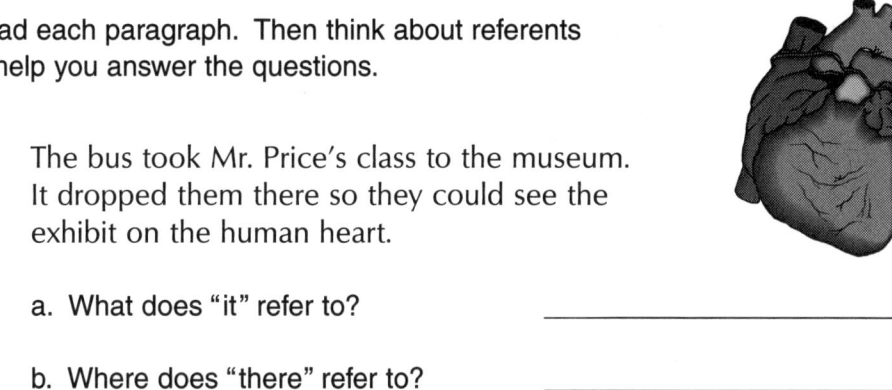

1. The bus took Mr. Price's class to the museum. It dropped them there so they could see the exhibit on the human heart.

    a. What does "it" refer to? _____

    b. Where does "there" refer to? _____

    c. Who do "them" and "they" refer to? _____

2. The boys wanted to see the tree with the arrow through it. The only way to get there was to walk on the trail. It was narrow and they were all scared to go alone.

    a. Where does "there" refer to? _____

    b. What was narrow? _____

    c. Who are "they"? _____

3. The soccer team won the state championship this year. They just took one game at a time until they won it all. That group of kids is really amazing!

    a. Who does "they" refer to? _____

    b. What does "it" refer to? _____

    c. Who is "that group of kids"? _____

4. "When you get home from school, you need to clean up the basement," Mom told Nate. "I went down there to find something. It was a mess from when Josh and Abe were here."

    a. Who does "you" refer to? _____

    b. Who does "I" refer to? _____

    c. Where is "there"? _____

Strategic Learning
Reading Comprehension: Level 2

Referents

Goal: Identify referents for gerunds and participial phrases

Circle the referent for the bold words in each sentence.

1. **Left unlocked**, the door swung wildly and banged against the barn.

2. **Snoring loudly**, the man in the theater disturbed everyone around him.

3. P.J. couldn't seem to get his work done. **Lying on the floor**, the fifth grader stared out the window with his book open next to him.

4. **Half baked**, the cookies were no good to anyone but the birds.

5. Bree was nervous. **Shaking like a leaf**, the aspiring actress got up on the stage.

6. **Frozen to the step**, the mitten was buried in ice.

7. Mr. Jones didn't feel well. **Collapsing in a heap**, the teacher fainted.

8. **Folded carefully**, the newspaper had become a hat.

9. **Reading aloud from the book**, the principal sat on the floor in front of the students.

10. **Having sat in the attic for years**, the old box was covered with dust.

11. **Thrilled to be chosen**, Rose proudly put the crown on her head.

12. **Sleeping quietly**, the baby stuck her thumb in her mouth.

Comparing and Contrasting

Instructor Information

> **Goal:** to understand and explain how things are alike and different
>
> **Objectives:** In this unit, your students will:
> - tell how things are alike
> - tell how things are different
> - use graphic organizers to compare things
> - identify what is being compared in sentences
> - identify words that signal similarities and differences
> - practice comparing things they read about

Comparing and contrasting require students to evaluate information. When students determine how items are alike and different, they are making judgments about the information. Identifying words that signal similarities and differences will help students comprehend what they read.

In this unit, students will tell how two things are alike and how two things are different. Once they can do that, they will compare items in other ways, such as using a Venn diagram. Students will also identify signal words that show comparisons.

Enrichment Activities

1. Bring in objects related to units your students are studying. For example, during a weather unit in science, bring in clothing to compare. Ask your students how a winter sweater and a jacket are alike and different or how sandals and boots compare. Write their responses in a chart on the board labeled *similarities* and *differences.*

2. Ask your students if they ever have trouble deciding what to eat in the cafeteria or at a restaurant. Explain how using comparison skills can help them decide. Demonstrate this idea by selecting two foods from the cafeteria menu, such as pizza and a ham sandwich. Write *Pizza* and *Ham Sandwich* across the top of a chart on the board. Along the left side, write questions to ask about each one, such as *How much does it cost? Is it served hot or cold? Have I eaten it lately? Do I like it?* and *Are we having it tonight at home?*

Comparing and Contrasting, *continued*

> Instructor Information

3. Enhance your students' understanding of the characters in a novel they're reading for class. Have your students choose two characters from the book to compare and write the characters' names in a Venn diagram. Then have your students list how the characters are alike and different according to traits like gender, age, personality, occupation, and values. For good writing practice, have each student follow up this comparison by writing a paragraph to summarize the comparison.

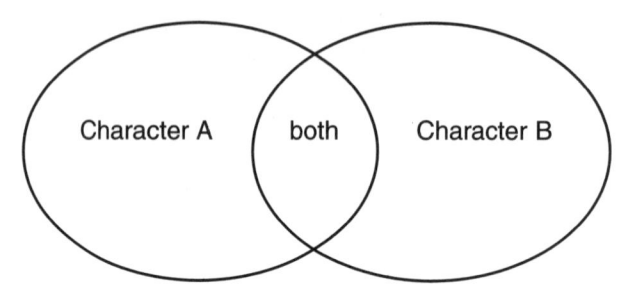

   Character A | both | Character B

4. Trying to decide which movie to watch is sometimes a challenge. Show your students how to facilitate this type of decision by comparing two movies. Select two current movies from the listing in your local paper or on the Internet. Write the movie titles at the top of a chart on the board. Write features to compare along the left side of the chart, such as *rating*, *type of movie*, *actors*, *times,* and *location*. Have your students fill in the chart and discuss their decisions about which movie to watch, based on their comparisons.

5. A class or school election is a perfect time for your students to practice their comparison skills. If your school doesn't hold elections, you might take advantage of a local, state, or national election. Ask your students to choose two candidates to compare. Make a chart on the board, listing the two candidates at the top. Next list qualities your students are interested in comparing down the left side of the chart, such as *experience*, *age*, *views on various topics*, etc. Then have your students vote for the candidate of their choice.

6. Selecting the right science project is sometimes a difficult task. To aid a student in decision-making, have her choose two projects to compare. Write the similarities and differences in a Venn diagram or chart. Compare features like *materials*, *cost*, *time*, *experience/knowledge*, *uniqueness*, and *enjoyment involved*. Then talk about the results to help the student choose which science project to complete.

7. Have your students look for two different ads for the same product in magazines and newspapers. Then ask your students to use a Venn diagram to compare the two ads for color, design, persuasiveness, size, and content. Ask volunteers to share what they found.

Comparing and Contrasting

Goal: compare and contrast how things are alike and different

To **compare** means to explain how two things are the **same**.
To **contrast** means to explain how two things are **different**.

A good way to compare and contrast things is to make a comparison chart. You write the details about each thing in the correct place in the chart. Here is an example chart. It shows how two weather conditions are alike and different.

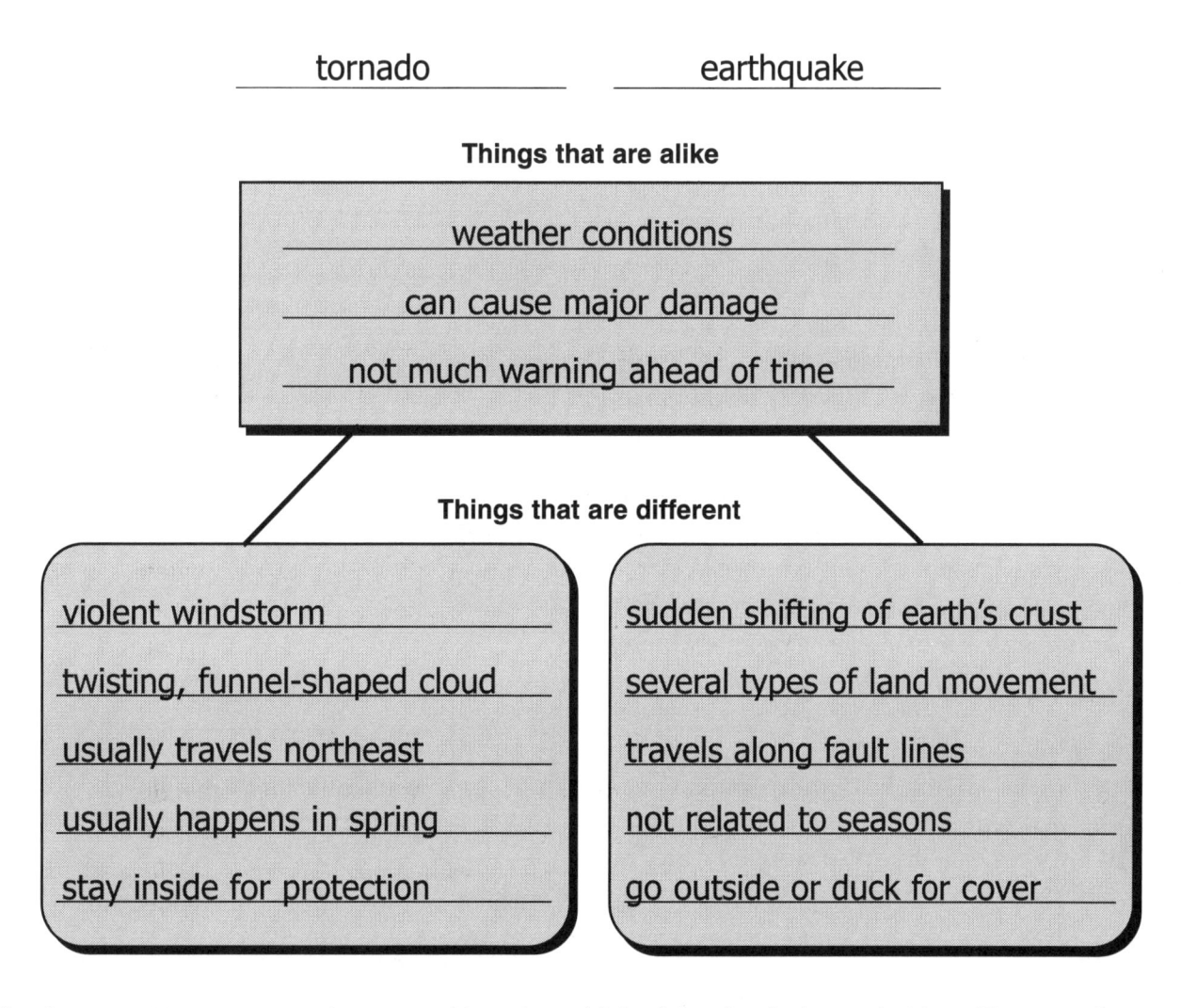

<u>　　　tornado　　　</u>　　　<u>　　earthquake　　</u>

Things that are alike

- weather conditions
- can cause major damage
- not much warning ahead of time

Things that are different

tornado	earthquake
violent windstorm	sudden shifting of earth's crust
twisting, funnel-shaped cloud	several types of land movement
usually travels northeast	travels along fault lines
usually happens in spring	not related to seasons
stay inside for protection	go outside or duck for cover

The first step to compare and contrast things is to think of the details for each thing. Then you can organize these details on a chart like this one.

Strategic Learning
Reading Comprehension: Level 2

Comparing and Contrasting

Goal: Identify items compared

Read each paragraph. Write what things are being compared and contrasted on the lines in the diagram.

1. Due to bad weather, all students will go home early. Students who walk home will be dismissed at 1:30 P.M. Students who ride busses will be dismissed at 2:00 P.M.

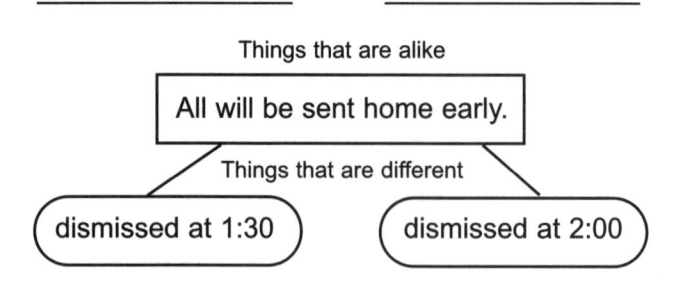

   Things that are alike
   All will be sent home early.
   Things that are different
   dismissed at 1:30
   dismissed at 2:00

2. After living in an apartment for several years, Shana's family moved to a house. The house is about the same size as their apartment, but Shana has her own bedroom. She doesn't have to share a room with her brother. They have a small backyard. They didn't have any yard at the apartment. The apartment was closer to the grocery store, however. Now Shana has to walk four blocks to get milk instead of just one block.

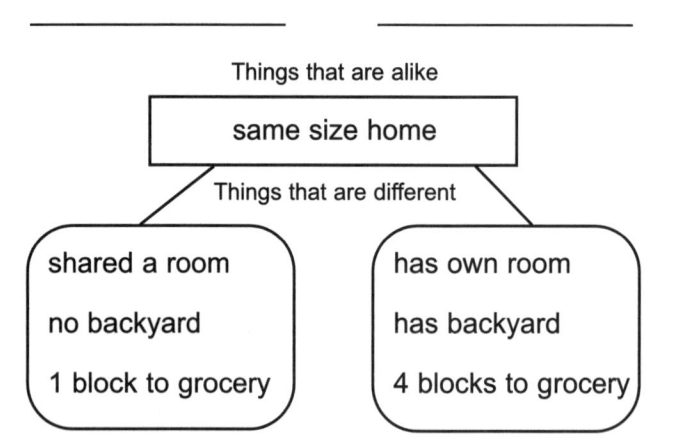

   Things that are alike
   same size home
   Things that are different
   shared a room
   no backyard
   1 block to grocery
   has own room
   has backyard
   4 blocks to grocery

3. Italian Marco Polo traveled by land to Asia when he was a teenager. Portugal's Prince Henry taught sailors how to explore by boat.

   Both men wanted to bring back riches from Asia. Marco Polo got there first. The stores in Italy sold the Asian goods at high prices. They also stopped other land explorers from getting to Asia.

   Prince Henry thought that he could find a water route to Asia. In 1497 one of his sailors discovered the water route to Asia. Now other European countries could sail to Asia and buy goods themselves.

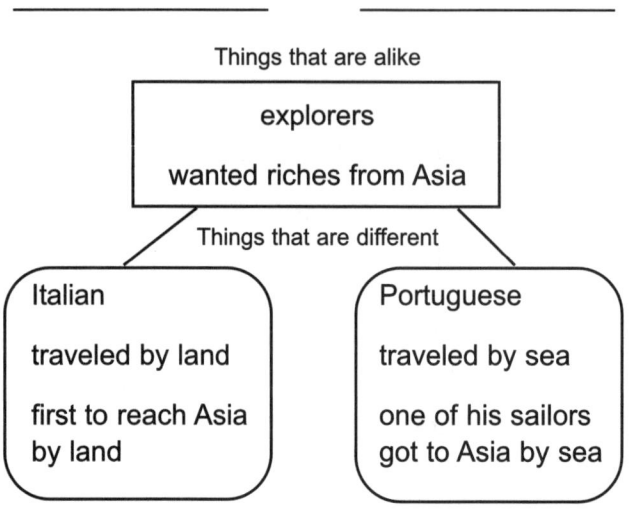

   Things that are alike
   explorers
   wanted riches from Asia
   Things that are different
   Italian
   traveled by land
   first to reach Asia by land
   Portuguese
   traveled by sea
   one of his sailors got to Asia by sea

90
Copyright © 2002 LinguiSystems, Inc.

Strategic Learning
Reading Comprehension: Level 2

Comparing and Contrasting

Goal: Compare and contrast

Look for these comparing and contrasting words in these passages. Fill in the chart for the first item. Then make your own chart for the second passage.

Comparing Words

just	like
same	also
both	too

Contrasting Words

however	rather
whereas	but
instead	than

1. Both a skateboard and roller skates are great for getting places in a hurry. Both have wheels, but you wear roller skates and stand on a skateboard. You can use both for doing cool stunts, but a skateboard is definitely better!

   _____ _____
   Things that are alike

   [chart with lines]

   Things that are different

   [two rounded boxes with lines]

2. Dan is an underwater explorer with the Mars and Stars Exploration Team. He is on assignment somewhere in the Milky Way. He puts on his wet suit and drops to the ocean floor.

   The first creature he sees is highly unusual. He is almost positive it is the rare dorkil! He checks his Mars and Stars Guide to extraterrestrial underwater creatures. Sure enough, it is a dorkil! The creature has the characteristic silver fins and copper-colored scales. It has a large mouth full of square teeth. The dorkil chases and eats small fish.

   Farther along, Dan discovers the frob. Like the dorkil, the frob lives only on the ocean floor. The frob is blue and as round as a ball. Unlike the dorkil, the frob has no skeleton. Instead of fins, it has long tentacles. The frob is a blob and catches its food by lying very still and waiting for small fish to swim by. Then it grabs them with its tentacles and stuffs them into its small, toothless mouth.

Strategic Learning
Reading Comprehension: Level 2

Comparing and Contrasting

Goal: Compare and contrast characters

Read this story. Look for words that signal comparisons or contrasts. Then complete the chart below to tell how the sisters were alike and how they were different from each other.

A Tale of Two Sisters

Once upon a time, Dot and Belle lived in a small one-bedroom apartment. Both of these sisters had long hair. Belle's was shining and silky, while Dot's was greasy and full of tangled knots. Belle's side of the room sparkled, shined, and smelled clean. However, Dot's side smelled like moldy cheese. Dot's pile of dirty underwear reached clear up to the ceiling. Eventually, Dot went mad because of Belle's nagging to clean up her mess. Belle moved to another apartment with a friend named Cinderella. Cinderella also liked to clean. They all lived happily ever after.

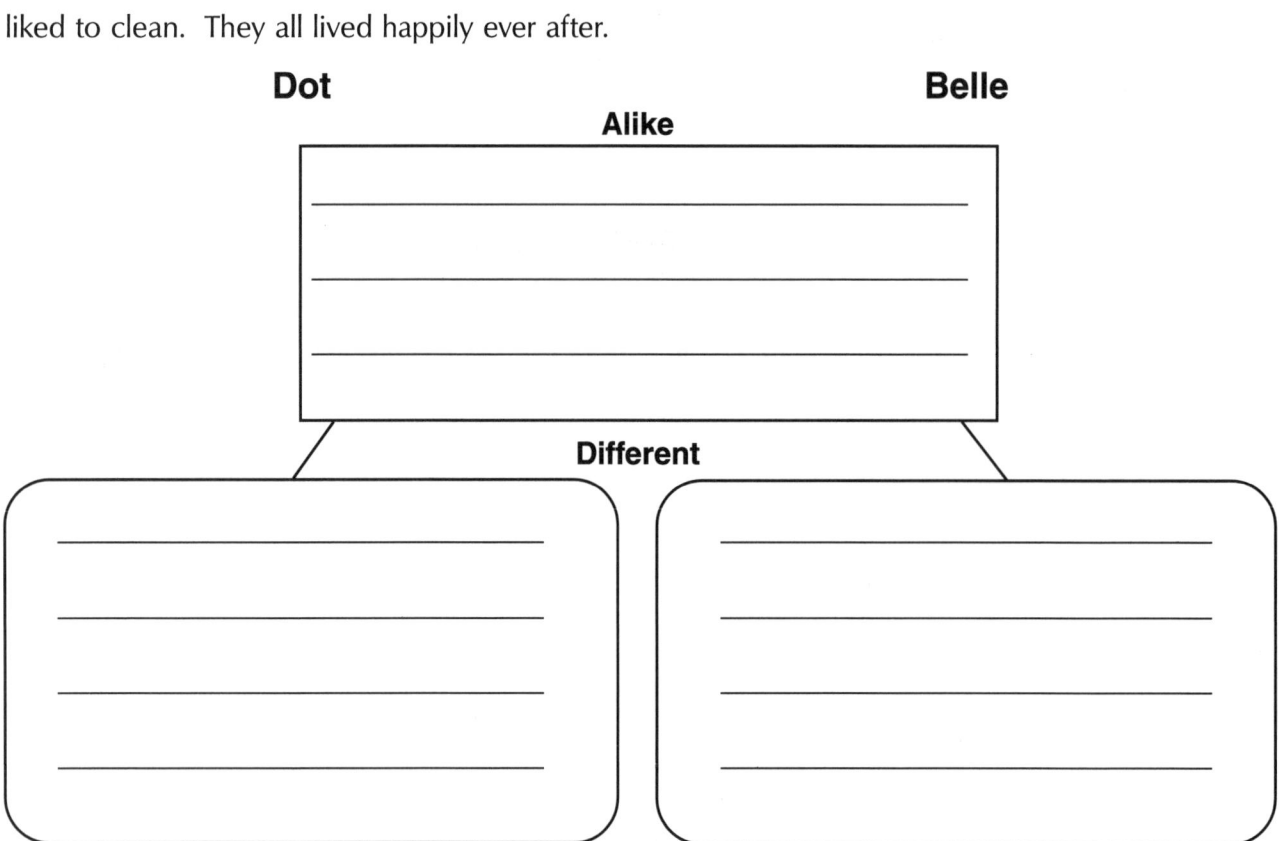

Dot   **Belle**

Alike

_____

_____

_____

Different

92
Copyright © 2002 LinguiSystems, Inc.

Strategic Learning
Reading Comprehension: Level 2

Comparing and Contrasting

Goal: Compare and contrast

Here are more words that signal how things are the same and different. Find these words in this paragraph and fill in the Venn diagram.

Comparing Words

both	like
similar	too
also	same
just	

Contrasting Words

however	rather
whereas	but
instead	than
while	let
instead of	words that end in **-er** or **-est**

Anthony and Silvia are brother and sister. Anthony is 14 years old and can be very serious. He is quiet in school, but after school, he likes to do things with his friends. His 11-year-old sister, Silvia, often tags along with Anthony and his friends. She tells funny stories and has a great imagination.

Both siblings get along well and have fun together. They have similar personalities and are well liked at school by the other students and by their teachers. Anthony would like to be a veterinarian someday and Silvia wants to be a pilot.

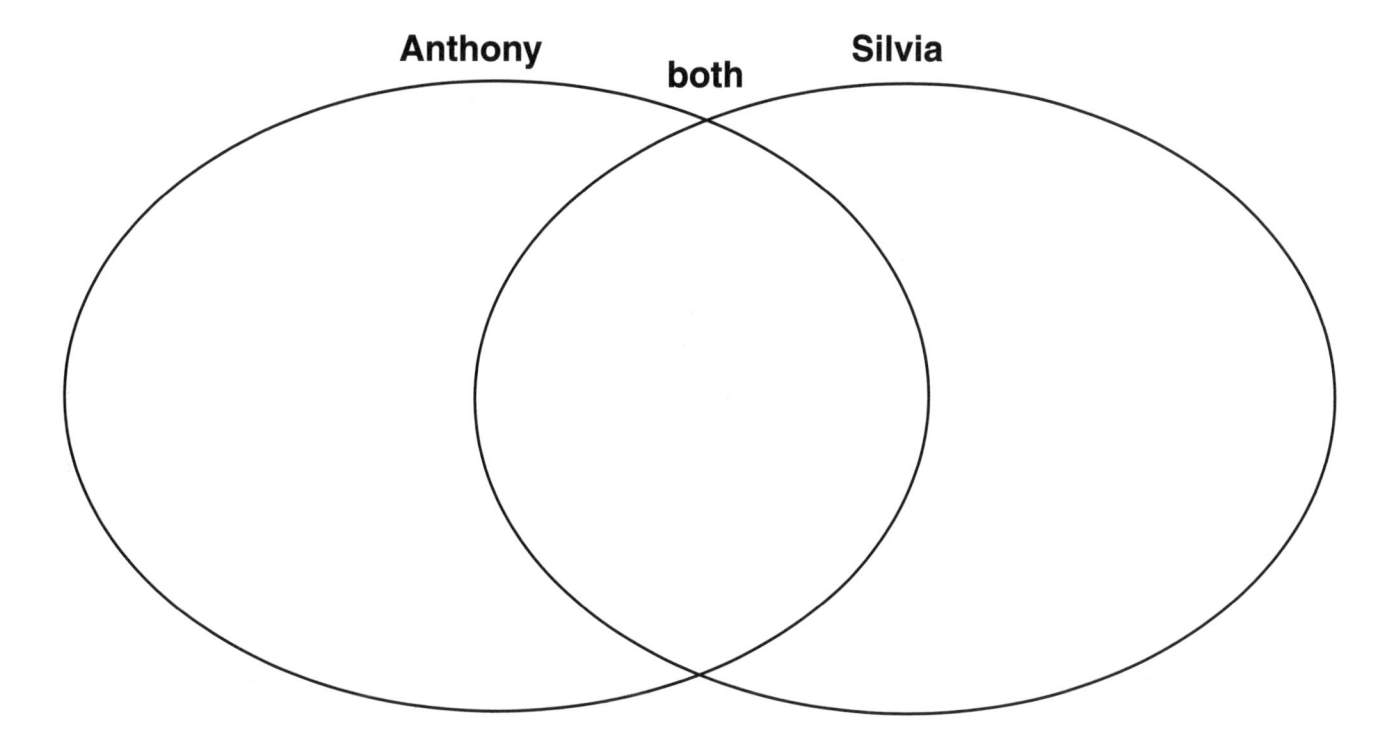

Anthony   both   **Silvia**

Comparing and Contrasting

Goal: Compare and contrast objects

Compare and contrast your choices before you buy something. That will help you decide which one to buy. Here are ads for two bikes. Use the information in the ads to fill in the chart below.

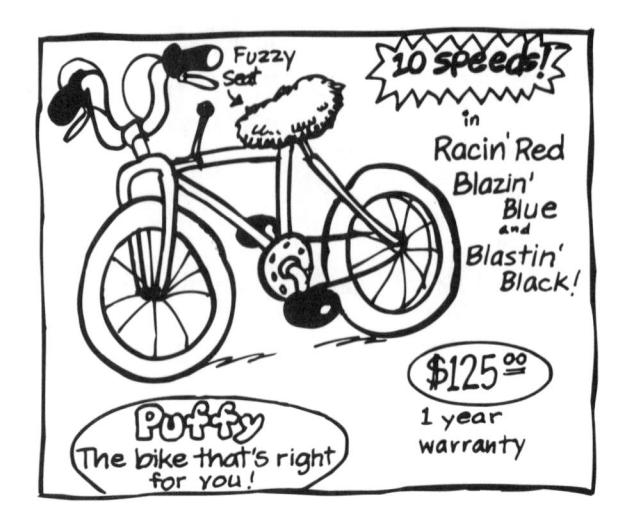

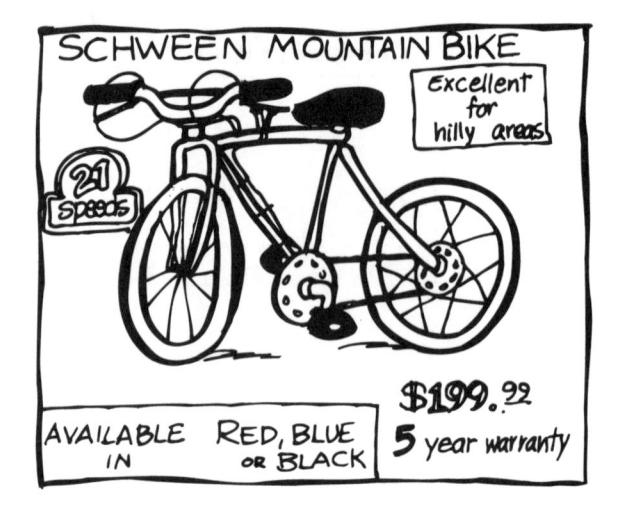

Puffy ad: Fuzzy Seat, 10 speeds!, in Racin' Red, Blazin' Blue and Blastin' Black! $125.00, 1 year warranty. Puffy — The bike that's right for you!

Schween Mountain Bike ad: Excellent for hilly areas, 21 speeds, Available in Red, Blue or Black, $199.99, 5 year warranty.

	Puffy	Schween
color		
price		
warranty		
speeds		
extra features		

Now you have compared and contrasted the two bikes. Write which one you would buy. Explain why.

_____

_____

94
Copyright © 2002 LinguiSystems, Inc.

Strategic Learning
Reading Comprehension: Level 2

Comparing and Contrasting

Goal: Compare and contrast groups of people

As you read this story, notice words that signal comparisons or contrasts. Then write how Aborigines and Native Americans are alike and different.

Aborigines and Native Americans

Aborigines and Native Americans have the same history in some ways. Both of these groups lived in tribes. They were the first people on their continents. Native Americans were the first people in America. Aborigines were the first people in Australia.

Later people from Europe came to America and Australia. They brought their diseases with them. These diseases killed many native people. Others were forced off their lands.

Today many Native Americans live on reservations. They practice their way of life there. Most Aborigines, though, do not live on reservations. Many of them have lost their traditions.

Aborigines **Native Americans**

Alike

_____
_____
_____
_____

Different

_____
_____
_____

_____
_____
_____

Strategic Learning
Reading Comprehension: Level 2

Copyright © 2002 LinguiSystems, Inc.

Comparing and Contrasting

Goal: Compare and contrast

Read this passage about Australia. Then fill in the diagram below to compare and contrast life in the outback with life in the cities.

Life in Australia

The outback is a vast area of land in Australia. The population is sparse there. Children are educated differently there than in the cities. Travel on outback roads is often difficult. Students can't easily walk or ride a bus to school. Many outback students attend school by mail or two-way radio.

The cities and the outback are alike in some ways. People in both places enjoy festivals and sports games. Rodeos are popular in the outback. Surfing and sailing are popular in the cities.

Outback   **Cities**

Things that are alike

Things that are different

Comparing and Contrasting

Goal: Compare and contrast

Read this story about the Iroquois Indians long ago. Then compare the way they lived to the way you live now.

The Iroquois Indians lived in what is now New York State and northern Pennsylvania. Early on their families lived in small houses or wigwams. These home were made of wood. Later they made larger houses called longhouses. These were also made from wood. Up to 12 families could live in one longhouse. Each family lived in a small compartment on one side of a center hallway. There were several longhouses in a village. A tall, wooden fence surrounded the village for protection.

Iroquois Indians **Me**

Alike

Different

Strategic Learning
Reading Comprehension: Level 2

97

Copyright © 2002 LinguiSystems, Inc.

Comparing and Contrasting

Goal: Compare and contrast characters

Read about Zero Man and Shockra. Then fill in the comparison diagram below.

Zero Man and Shockra

Both Zero Man and Shockra are superheroes. They are also married to each other. They use their special powers to fight evil and crime in Metro City.

These defenders of justice have different backgrounds. Zero Man was born and raised on Earth. Shockra, on the other hand, was born on the planet Junga.

Zero Man and Shockra are both powerful, but their powers are different. Zero Man can disappear and reappear in any place. He also has a special "truth shield" that forces criminals to tell the truth.

Shockra is more powerful than Zero Man. She can generate electricity in her body and destroy her enemies with shock waves. She can fly faster than a jet. Her most amazing ability, though, is that she can see the future. Shockra knows when danger is near. She senses who will commit a crime, so she and Zero Man can plan ahead.

Zero Man   **Shockra**

Things that are alike

_____
_____
_____

Things that are different

_____   _____
_____   _____
_____   _____

Comparing and Contrasting

Goal: Compare and contrast

Part of what makes reading fun is creating a picture in your mind of what you read. Describe how you picture each passage below in your mind. Then compare and contrast your images with a partner.

1. I had put the garbage out for the trash collector. Later I saw a large dog nosing through the garbage. I almost pulled my hair out! This dog was dragging banana peels and eggshells all over my front yard.

    How do you think the person talking looks?

    _____

    Describe the dog.

    _____

    Describe the yard and the neighborhood.

    _____

2. You can't find your math book and remember seeing your little brother practicing his circus act by balancing it on his head. You go to his bedroom and slowly open the door. You can't believe your eyes. It's the biggest mess you've ever seen!

    Describe your image of this passage.

    _____

    _____

    _____

3. Karen and Laura waited in line to ride the Super Triple Loop roller coaster. Finally they got in a cart and the attendant belted them in. The cart moved slowly up the steep track and paused for a moment at the top. Then WHOOSH, down it went! Karen was laughing. She threw her arms in the air and whooped for joy. Laura hung on for dear life and didn't open her eyes until the ride stopped.

    Describe your image of this passage.

    _____

    _____

    _____

Strategic Learning
Reading Comprehension: Level 2

Comparing and Contrasting

Goal: Understand figurative comparisons

Sometimes writers use similes or metaphors to compare two things that do not seem to be alike at all. The writer finds something that is the same about the two things.

A **metaphor** says one thing is the same as another thing. Here's an example comparing a river and a snake.

The river is a snake, winding through the valley.

A **simile** uses the words **like** or **as** to compare two things. Here's an example comparing snow and a blanket.

The snow was like a blanket across the field.

The sentences below use metaphors or similes to compare things. Underline the things being compared in each sentence. Then tell how these things are the same.

1. The tornado was like a jazz dancer, twisting through the fields.

   _____

2. Juan's suitcase was an anchor, slowing him down.

   _____

3. Kim's fastball is like a speeding bullet.

   _____

4. Kathy's prom dress is as billowy as a cloud.

   _____

5. Blake is a clam when it comes to secrets.

   _____

6. Camels are the ships of the desert.

   _____

Comparing and Contrasting

Goal: Understand figurative comparisons

Look at the things being compared in these metaphors. Fill in the chart to tell how they are different and alike.

I shoveled snow for two hours. My feet were blocks of ice.

The fog around the bridge was pea soup.

Charlie always picks on his little sister. He has a heart of stone.

Kim is a bear when she wakes up in the morning.

Julia's sweater was a spring rainbow.

	Different	**Alike**
feet ice blocks		
fog pea soup		
heart stone		
Kim bear		
sweater spring rainbow		

Strategic Learning
Reading Comprehension: Level 2

Comparing and Contrasting

Goal: Write comparisons and contrasts

Use comparing and contrasting signal words to complete this assignment. Write at least one comparing and one contrasting sentence about the following items. An example is done for you.

two sports: soccer, basketball
compare: Both soccer and basketball players wear uniforms.
contrast: You kick a soccer ball, but you shoot a basketball.

Two music groups: _____ and _____

Compare: _____

_____

Contrast: _____

_____

Two restaurants: _____ and _____

Compare: _____

_____

Contrast: _____

_____

Two video games: _____ and _____

Compare: _____

_____

Contrast: _____

_____

Two books: _____ and _____

Compare: _____

_____

Contrast: _____

_____

Comparing and Contrasting

Goal: Compare and contrast characters

Read this conversation between Celia and her grandma. Then make a comparison chart to show the similarities and differences between these two people.

"I'm tired of walking to school," Celia complained. "It's almost a mile away!"

Grandma smiled. "Celia, at your age, I walked two miles to school each day."

"You're kidding!" said Celia with astonishment. "Really?"

"In those days, most everyone lived on a farm and the schoolhouse was in town. We didn't have a bus and no one had a car. I walked two miles, but some of my friends walked even farther. My sisters and I got up early because we had chores to do before school started. My sisters and I would walk to school with our lunch buckets."

"Why didn't you eat the school lunch?" asked Celia.

"I went to a one-room school and we didn't have a cafeteria. We only had 15 students in the whole school," replied Grandma.

"Only 15 students? My class is twice as big as your whole school, Grandma. How many were in your grade?" asked Celia.

"There were two in my grade besides me," said Grandma. "We had only one teacher for all the grades, too."

"What did your teacher do?" Celia asked.

"She gave us our assignments at the beginning of the day and we worked on them while she worked with other students. When I was in the upper grades, I got to help younger students learn their lessons," Grandma explained.

"That sounds like my class. My teacher gives us our assignments in the morning and then she works with different groups of kids. Sometimes I get to read to the kindergarten class." Celia smiled. "But I'm really glad I don't have to walk two miles to school every day!"

Strategic Learning
Reading Comprehension: Level 2

Fact and Opinion

Instructor Information

> **Goal:** to understand and identify fact and opinion in a variety of reading passages
>
> **Objectives:** In this unit, your students will:
> - understand the difference between fact and opinion
> - use clue words to identify facts and opinions
> - identify facts and opinions in newspaper advertisements and dialog
> - use facts and opinions to persuade others
> - identify facts and opinions in a movie review
> - use fact and opinions to write a review

Understanding the difference between fact and opinion requires students to make judgments about what they read. Students need to know that word clues can help them identify fact vs. opinion.

In this unit, students will understand the difference between fact and opinion. The identification of certain clue words will help students successfully recognize the difference between facts and opinions in a variety of reading passages. Students will also use facts and opinions to persuade others as well as understand that opinions can change when new information is introduced. Final tasks in this section require students to apply their knowledge of fact and opinion in a variety of writing tasks.

Enrichment Activities

1. Have your students collect several statements from print advertisements. The phrases they collect might express thoughts such as "the best way to spend a summer's day" or "made by hand." Separate the statements into facts and opinions. Talk about the merits of using each in advertising.

2. Strengthen the concept of fact and opinion by asking your students, "Is it harder or easier to argue with someone who is always stating his opinions rather than facts?" Use their answers to frame a discussion about how opinions alone do not create

Fact and Opinion, *continued*

Instructor Information

strong arguments or positions. Lead them to understand that facts are essential to persuading another person to your point of view.

3. Write a single item on the board, such as *rap music*. Then have your students brainstorm and label fact and opinion statements that include the item. For example, they might say, "Drums are an important part of rap music" and label it as a fact.

4. Play a "fact and opinion" game show. Separate your students into two teams. Have a member of each team take turns "squaring off" against one another. Read a statement to the two contestants. The first person to correctly label the statement as a fact or an opinion gets a point for her team.

5. Write an opinion statement on the board, such as "Everyone needs to know how to expertly use a computer." Ask your students to brainstorm some fact statements that would either support or argue against the opinion statement. They might not know exact statistics to cite, but they could brainstorm the type of fact statements, such as "Only a small percentage people need to be expert computer users for their jobs" or "Computers are much easier to use today than they used to be, so you don't have to be an expert."

6. Have your students compare and contrast a front page article in a newspaper and an opinion column. Help them identify the words and phrases that are characteristic of fact and opinion statements.

7. Have students prepare brief persuasive speeches on a topic of their choosing (*why a certain music group is better than another* or *why you should eat at a particular restaurant*, for example). Encourage them to use a mixture of fact and opinion statements in their presentations.

Fact and Opinion

Goal: understand the difference between fact and opinion statements

People around you use facts and opinions to persuade you to agree with them. Advertisers use facts and opinions to make you want to buy their products. If you know the difference between facts and opinions, you can make better decisions for yourself.

Here are some things you need to know about facts and opinions.

- A **fact** is something you can **prove**. Facts are true statements. Here are some facts.

    This package weighs ten pounds.

    The lamp requires a 60-watt bulb.

    The stadium was sold out for the championship game.

FACT

something you can **prove**

Notice that facts often contain statistics or details that can easily be proven.

- An **opinion** is how someone **feels** or **thinks** about something. Opinions may or may not be proven. Here are some opinions.

    This package seems really heavy.

    I don't think that lamp is bright enough.

    I believe I can find a ticket for the game somewhere.

OPINION

what you **think** or **feel**

Notice that opinions often contain words like these.

seems	think	believe	best	worst
best	all	many	better	awful

- Watch Out! Some statements are mixed. They contain both a fact and an opinion. Underline the fact part of this statement and circle the opinion part.

    Some flowers aren't very colorful, and dull flowers are boring.

106
Copyright © 2002 LinguiSystems, Inc.

Strategic Learning
Reading Comprehension: Level 2

Fact and Opinion

Goal: Identify fact and opinion statements and clue words

Read each statement. Write *F* it is a fact and *O* if it is an opinion. Circle the words that help you make your decision.

1. _____ I think roses are the most beautiful flowers.

2. _____ Nearly 40% of Americans still smoke cigarettes.

3. _____ This has been the warmest winter on record.

4. _____ Spring will probably be hotter than normal.

5. _____ Your research report must be ten pages long.

6. _____ Well-dressed people are usually very nice.

7. _____ More people in the world attend soccer games than any other sport.

8. _____ Our basketball team is going to be awful this year.

9. _____ An average computer lasts for three-and-a-half years.

10. _____ It's horrible to use a computer if you can't type well.

11. _____ The downtown library probably has just what you're looking for.

12. _____ This muggy weather seems to make me sleepy.

13. _____ The salesperson said I must pay by cash or check.

14. _____ The cafeteria food seems to taste better today than it did yesterday.

15. _____ We could avoid 80% percent of all head injuries if people wore protective headgear.

Strategic Learning
Reading Comprehension: Level 2

Fact and Opinion

Goal: Write fact and opinion statements

Read each fact statement. Reword the sentence so it expresses an opinion on the same topic. An example is done for you.

1. Fact: The grocery store runs out of bananas every Sunday.

   Opinion: *The grocery store should order more bananas.*

2. Fact: That music store sells more hip-hop CDs than any other kind of music.

   Opinion: _____

3. Fact: A TV uses a lot more power than a light bulb does.

   Opinion: _____

Read each opinion statement. Reword the sentence so it is a fact.

4. Opinion: There is nothing better than cereal for breakfast.

   Fact: _____

5. Opinion: The piano is the easiest instrument to learn.

   Fact: _____

6. Opinion: Rainy days are always depressing.

   Fact: _____

108
Copyright © 2002 LinguiSystems, Inc.

Strategic Learning
Reading Comprehension: Level 2

Fact and Opinion

Goal: Identify facts and opinions in a dialog

Conversation is often a mixture of facts and opinions. Read the interview between a sports reporter and football quarterback Hank Barris. Underline each fact and circle each opinion. Some of the statements aren't clearly fact or opinion. Share your decisions with other students and see if you all agreed. Talk about why you labeled some of the statements the way you did.

Reporter: Well, Hank, how many games will the Cats win this year?

Hank Barris: Oh, I don't know. We'll probably win at least ten.

Reporter: Wow! Your fans would be thrilled.

Hank Barris: You know, we only pulled out three victories last year. We think we can do better this time around.

Reporter: How's your arm feeling?

Hank Barris: I had surgery on my elbow last winter. It's getting stronger. I'll probably come back even stronger this year.

Reporter: And how about that new contract? You're making a lot of money for a quarterback on a losing team, aren't you?

Hank Barris: It might seem like I'm making way too much money. The contract says I get paid ten million whether we win or not. Of course, winning would be better than losing.

Reporter: Is it true that you're giving a lot of money to charities these days, too?

Hank Barris: I like to think I'm giving something back to the community. I do have three foundations that I support.

Reporter: Well, Hank, here's to a great season.

Hank Barris: We're going to have a lot of fun this year.

Strategic Learning
Reading Comprehension: Level 2

Fact and Opinion

Goal: Identify facts and opinions in advertisements

Read each newspaper advertisement. Decide which part of the statement is fact and which is opinion. Write the statements on the appropriate lines.

① SCRUB & SHINE

Scrub and Shine floor polish dries in only 5 minutes. You'll never need to wait for a glorious shine again!

Fact: _____

Opinion: _____

② Flawless Face

Flawless Face fights acne with two chemically balanced ingredients. You'll have the clearest skin ever!

Fact: _____

Opinion: _____

③ The Soccer Hut

No one offers you selections like **The Soccer Hut**! Come in soon for our spring sale, 25% off all merchandise.

Fact: _____

Opinion: _____

④ TRADING POST

You'll find all you need for sports card trading at the **Trading Post**. Stop by our new store at 2500 West 176th Street today!

Fact: _____

Opinion: _____

Fact and Opinion

> Goal: Use fact and opinion to persuade an audience

Create a magazine advertisement for one of the topics below. Use both facts and opinions in your ad. Once you've chosen your topic, list some facts and opinions about what you're trying to sell.

Facts about your item might include what it's made of, what it includes, what color it is, or what it does. Opinions might include statements such as "It's the greatest of its kind" or "You can't be without it."

After you've brainstormed facts and opinions, create your advertisement on another sheet of paper. Look at ads in magazines to get some ideas about designing your ad.

What you're advertising:
- ❑ latest CD by your favorite group
- ❑ movie
- ❑ TV show
- ❑ athletic shoes
- ❑ pet food
- ❑ snack chips
- ❑ soft drink
- ❑ hair care product

Facts   **Opinions**

_____   _____

_____   _____

_____   _____

_____   _____

_____   _____

Fact and Opinion

Goal: Identify fact and opinion in a movie review

Reviews include a mixture of fact and opinion. Read this movie review and complete the chart below with facts and opinions from the review.

Harry Porter and the Sordid Stone

This movie clocks in at just under two hours long. It was probably the longest two hours of my life. Martin Carter, director of *Triassic Park*, also directs this movie. I'm not sure which movie is more horrible.

The story begins with twelve-year-old Harry Porter's first day at a new school. On the way to school, he meets a talking stone. A talking stone might be the worst idea for a character I've ever seen. I'd tell you the rest of the story, but you'd probably be bored with it. I know I was.

The director used a cast of over one thousand children in this movie. Most people will at least admire him for that. The movie had a budget of nearly one hundred million dollars. I don't think I've ever seen a bigger waste of money in my life.

Harry Porter and the Sordid Stone is playing at the Valley Green Cinema starting Friday. You might enjoy it, but I doubt it.

Facts	Opinions
_____	_____
_____	_____
_____	_____
_____	_____
_____	_____

Fact and Opinion

Goal: Use fact and opinion to write a review

Plan a review for a book you've recently read or a TV show or movie you've seen. Write at least five facts and five opinion statements about what you're reviewing. Then write your review on another sheet of paper.

Title: _____

Facts	Opinions
1. _____	1. _____
2. _____	2. _____
3. _____	3. _____
4. _____	4. _____
5. _____	5. _____

Summarizing

> **Goal:** to summarize information in a reading passage
>
> **Objectives:** In this unit, your students will:
> - use a diagram to plan a summary
> - ask questions to summarize information
> - paraphrase information to summarize it
> - write one-sentence summaries
> - paraphrase and summarize reading passages

Instructor Information

When students first learn to summarize, they usually write either too much or too little information. Sometimes they simply repeat the information word-for-word. It takes guided practice for students to master the skill of summarizing by paraphrasing, keeping just the important information and omitting the details.

The activities in this unit will teach students to summarize appropriately. They will learn to pull out the main idea and include only key details. They will use key words and phrases, break larger ideas into more specific ideas, and include just enough information in their summaries to convey the gist of what they have read.

Enrichment Activities

1. Use a graphic such as the one below to help students summarize.

Summarizing, continued

> Instructor Information

2. Have students underline or highlight important information as they read.

3. Teach students the difference between summarizing and paraphrasing by showing the amount of detail (or lack of it) between the two.

4. Have students read the same paragraph to themselves. Then have them write summaries and read them aloud. If they've answered the *who, what, when, where, why,* and *how* questions without providing any unnecessary detail, they get six slips of paper with their names on them to drop in a lottery box. After the whole group has read their summaries, draw the lottery winner's name from the box. Give the winner a prize.

5. Get a discussion going on the importance of summarizing. When is summarizing crucial? When is it convenient? When isn't it appropriate?

6. Give your students a clear signal when you're summarizing information, such as, "So, to summarize what we learned today, . . ." It may help students to remember summarizing starters like, "The most important thing . . . ." or "The main thing we talked about was . . . ."

7. Divide students into small groups. Have them make lists of words or phrases containing summary words or starters. Then have them make lists of words or phrases containing paraphrasing words or starters. Compare lists as a group.

8. Read a short passage, perhaps two or three paragraphs, to the group. Give students a copy to read along with you, too. After the reading, have them write a summary about what you just read. Have students compare one summary to another.

9. Have students read a short passage and underline the important information as they read. When they're finished reading, have them turn their papers over and write summaries based on what they remember underlining. Have them go back and forth between the passage and their summaries until they're satisfied they have only written pertinent information in their summaries. If they have trouble with this (and they probably will!), have them reduce the passage the first time to one paragraph, the second time to a few sentences, and the last time to one sentence.

10. Tell your students they are going to place an ad or send a telegram. Each word costs ten cents. Tell them they can spend $2 to send the message. Have a folder of articles for them to summarize in up to 20 words.

Summarizing

Goal: learn how to summarize information in a reading passage

Summarizing is a tough skill to learn, but it is an absolutely essential skill. Summarizing helps you remember what you read and condense the information to share it with other people.

Here's what to do to summarize what you read.

- **Ask yourself questions.** Ask **who**, **what**, **when**, **where**, **why**, and **how** questions to pick out the most important information. Remember that in a summary, you may not need to use all of these questions to find the important information.

    Who are the characters in the passage?

    What is the main idea or problem?

    When is it happening?

    Where is it happening?

    Why are the characters doing what they're doing?

    How was the problem resolved?

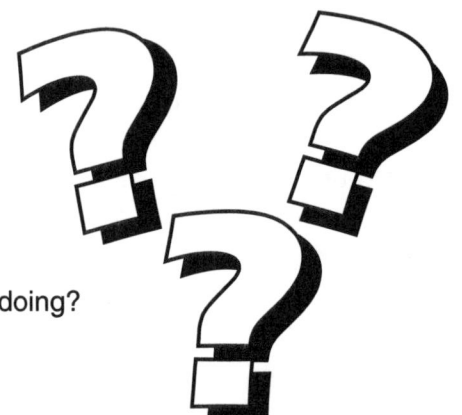

- **Write just ONE sentence** to summarize what you read.

- **Leave out details that aren't important.**

- **Check your ONE sentence again.** Does it have only essential information?

Here's how to summarize the phone message below using only ONE sentence.

"Hi, Joleen, this is Kendra. The movie starts at 7:30 tonight, so my mom will pick you up around 6:45. I know it'll be a great movie. I think Thea will go, too. See you later!"

Summary: Kendra's mom will pick you up at 6:45 for the 7:30 movie.

Summarizing

Goal: Use a diagram to plan a summary

A summary diagram is a plan to organize information to write a summary. Remember that not all the answers to the questions are vital to every summary. Use this diagram to summarize what you read.

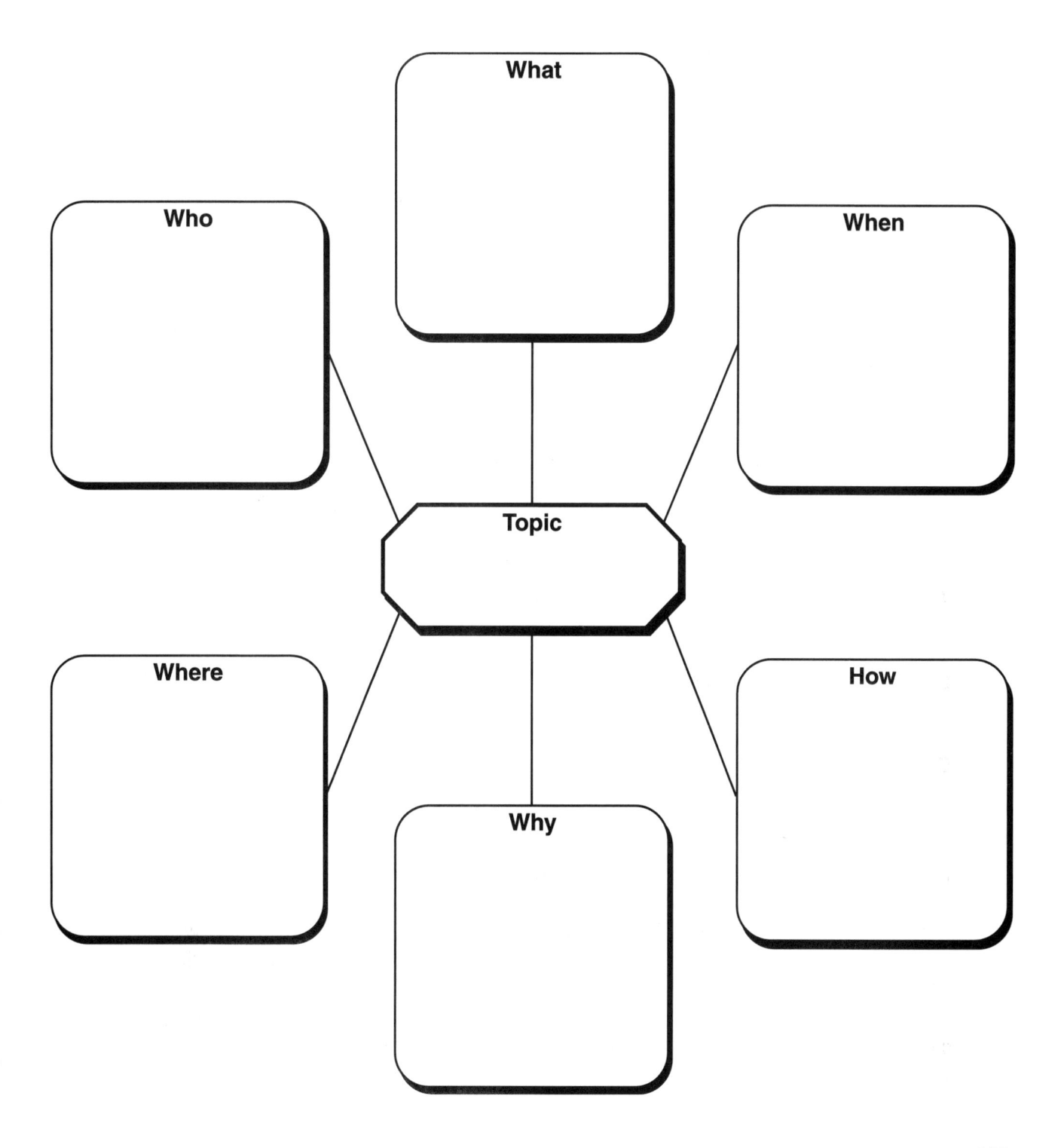

What

Who

When

Topic

Where

How

Why

Strategic Learning
Reading Comprehension: Level 2

Summarizing

Goal: Answer questions to summarize

Read this passage. Then answer the questions. Put a check by each question that is vital to a summary of the passage. Cross out the questions that are not important for a summary. Then summarize this passage in one sentence.

The Saguaro

What grows in the desert, is 60 feet tall, and lives 150 years? A saguaro cactus!

Saguaro cacti are the largest cacti in the southwestern United States. Their trunks grow to be over two-and-a-half feet wide. Each giant cactus weighs more than two elephants combined.

The saguaro is a valuable food source. Local Native Americans use the flesh, seeds, and juice of the saguaro. Many desert creatures also enjoy saguaro fruit. One saguaro fruit can have up to 4,000 seeds. These seeds are spread when the fruit opens, right before the rainy season begins.

The Saguaro National Monument in Arizona is home to many of these huge and beautiful cacti. If you visit there, don't expect to see these plants change overnight. The saguaro is one of the slowest-growing plants in the world, taking over 30 years to form its first branch.

1. Who likes the saguaro cactus? _____
2. What is special about saguaro cacti? _____
   _____
3. Where does the saguaro cactus grow? _____
4. When do saguaro fruits ripen and open? _____
5. Why does it take a long time to see any changes in a saguaro cactus? _____
6. How long does it take a saguaro to grow its first arm? _____

Write your summary of this passage in one sentence.

_____

_____

Summarizing

Goal: Paraphrase and summarize

When you put a whole message in your own words without shortening it, you are paraphrasing. When you condense a whole message into one short sentence, you are summarizing.

Read the passages below. First paraphrase each passage. Then summarize each passage in one sentence.

> "This is a severe weather warning. Dangerous thunderstorms with high winds gusting out of the north at 55 miles per hour have been sighted just 25 miles from the airport. All flights have been cancelled and travelers are advised to stay in the terminal until the storm has passed."

Paraphrase

_____

_____

_____

Summary sentence

_____

> Learning can be hard and learning can be fun.
> I know that it's much easier once it has begun.
> Learning stretches my brain, though I can't see it grow.
> I can tell that I am smarter by the new things that I know.

Paraphrase

_____

_____

_____

Summary sentence

_____

Summarizing

Goal: Use one sentence to summarize

Write one sentence to summarize each passage below.

Our Hero

Aaron was a hero today. Through his binoculars, he saw a small train of gray smoke rising from a dense thicket of trees. Fire! In his lookout station, he called the fire department. Aaron told them the exact location of the fire. The fire department responded in about five minutes and extinguished the blaze in a flash.

1. Summary: _____

The Roadrunner

The roadrunner isn't just a cartoon character. It's a real bird that lives in the desert. When it's hungry, it runs all around trying to find lizards, grasshoppers, snakes, and spiders. A roadrunner can run 25 miles per hour. You can often see it chasing after a jack rabbit, but the roadrunner isn't trying to catch the rabbit. It's trying to catch the insects the speedy rabbit scares out of hiding as it runs past.

2. Summary: _____

Native Americans

The Mandan were one of the many Native American groups who lived on the Great Plains in what is known as North Dakota. They lived in villages in houses called earth lodges because they were made entirely of mud and thatch. They were prairie farmers who raised maize, sunflowers, and squash. They fished and hunted buffalo and other game for meat and hides for clothing. Nothing from a successful hunt was ever wasted.

3. Summary: _____

Summarizing

Goal: Summarize and paraphrase

Read each passage. Write a short, one-sentence summary. Then write a paraphrase of each passage in your own words.

In the News

Tyrone is a photographer for a small newspaper. He has worked there for the past six years. He takes pictures of everything from sporting events to rock concerts, from social events to county fairs. Last year Tyrone won an award for his photograph of a tornado lifting the roof from a house. He loves the variety of things he gets to see and do.

1. Summary: _____

2. Paraphrase: _____

A Healthy Alert

Today the newspaper ran an article about teen health. The article said that more and more teens are dying every year from heart disease. Medical studies show that many teens have dangerous fatty deposits around their hearts. The article said that too little exercise and unhealthy diets are to blame.

3. Summary: _____

4. Paraphrase: _____

Strategic Learning
Reading Comprehension: Level 2

121

Copyright © 2002 LinguiSystems, Inc.

Summarizing

Goal: Summarize and paraphrase

Read each passage. Write a short, one-sentence summary. Then write a paraphrase of each passage in your own words.

Headline Hits

The copyeditor at some newspapers is in charge of writing headlines. The editor must write a clever headline that will catch the attention of readers. This task can be difficult because the headline has to be the right number of letters to fit the space above the story.

1. Summary: _____
   _____

2. Paraphrase: _____
   _____
   _____
   _____

Heavy!

There are two reasons newspaper printing presses are almost always found on the ground floor of a building. First, the press itself is very large and heavy. Second, each roll of paper sent through the press weighs close to a ton. A large newspaper may use more than 250 tons of paper per day.

3. Summary: _____
   _____

4. Paraphrase: _____
   _____
   _____
   _____

Summarizing

Goal: Use key information to summarize

Underline the key information in each passage. Then write a one-sentence summary about each one.

The Laughing Hyena

Contrary to its name, the laughing hyena really isn't jolly! It has a reputation for being a scavenger that steals other animals' goods and eats all of what it kills, including the bones. African legend also says that the hyena can imitate the voice of a man and will lure a person away from his tribe to be attacked by the pack. In fact, hyenas are so cowardly, they only hunt in packs.

1. Summary: _____

The Koala

The koala is an Australian mammal with no tail; round ears; and soft, thick fur. The koala is sometimes called a bear but is not a bear at all. It's a marsupial. Like the kangaroo, the female koala gives birth to an underdeveloped offspring, which she then carries in a pouch on her stomach until it develops completely. Koalas aren't fussy eaters. They eat leaves and stems of eucalyptus trees and hardly ever drink water. In fact, the word *koala* means "no drink" in Australian Aborigine.

2. Summary: _____

Jogging

Jogging is great aerobic exercise that fits into just about anyone's budget and schedule. The only equipment you need is loose-fitting clothing and well-cushioned running shoes. You can jog just about anywhere at any time of year because many cities have indoor running tracks. Just be safe. Don't run when it's dark and try to run with a partner.

3. Summary: _____

Summarizing

Goal: Summarize to make an ad

Advertisers take a lot of information about a product or service and write it in a small amount of space. They summarize. Read the passage about a new line of guitars. Then create an ad that summarizes the information someone would need to know to buy the guitar.

> The Gibson Company has been making guitars for over 75 years, and their latest guitars will ensure their success for many years to come. These instruments are unique for two reasons—their looks and their prices.
>
> The Gibson "Plaid Plucker" model sells for just $249.95. This is the first plaid guitar ever made and is perfect for the beginner as well as professionals.
>
> Another star in the Gibson line-up is the "Strum-vation." This cherry-red beauty gives you the option of plugging into an amp and really turning up the volume. It sells for $449.95.
>
> Gibson is the guitar company to trust because each instrument is designed, built, and tested by guitar players.

Now create your ad.

Summarizing

> **Goal:** Use questions to proofread a summary

Read a newspaper or magazine article. Underline only important information. Then write a summary of the article below.

Article Headline: _____

Publication: _____

Author: _____

Summary: _____

_____

_____

_____

Share your summary with a partner. Check your summaries with this checklist. Make any needed corrections in your summaries.

1. Is the summary in the writer's own words?   yes   no

2. Is the most important information presented first?   yes   no

3. Were only the most important details included?   yes   no

4. Were the most important characters named?   yes   no

5. Did the writer clearly state the main idea or problem?   yes   no

6. Were both the conflict and its resolution mentioned?   yes   no

Strategic Learning
Reading Comprehension: Level 2

Inferences

Instructor Information

> **Goal:** to use clues to make inferences about what is happening in stories, pictures, and everyday events
>
> **Objectives:** In this unit, your students will:
>
> - read stories and make inferences about what happened
> - use context clues to infer the meanings of words
> - make inferences about passages or characters
> - change their inferences based on new information

Making inferences requires students to use logical thinking skills as they evaluate information and make judgments. Students need to know that word and story clues can help them make inferences about what is happening in a story or what a character will say or do. More importantly, perhaps, making inferences is an important life skill. Making inferences helps us to avoid dangerous situations, understand what is happening around us, and be more adept in social situations.

In this unit, students will use available information and their own experiences to make inferences in a variety of situations. Students will make inferences about stories, characters, and everyday events. New information will give students an opportunity to change their predictions.

Enrichment Activities

1. Cut out photographs from newspapers or magazines and bring them to your class. Show the pictures and ask students to supply the following information by using both inference and their imaginations.

    character(s)

    the setting

    what is happening

2. Find a piece of dialog in a play between two people. Give your students copies of the dialog, but omit the speaking parts of one of the characters. Have your students read this one-sided conversation and supply fitting dialog for the other character.

Inferences, *continued*

> Instructor Information

3. Explain to your students that they make inferences all day long. Inferences help them successfully complete their daily activities. For example, they might know that it's almost time for lunch because they are feeling hungry, they can smell food from the cafeteria, or people are starting to put their books away.

   How do you know when each of these things is happening or is about to happen?

   Your teacher wants the class to be quiet.

   Your parent is really proud of you.

   You are doing well on a test.

   A friend is angry with you.

   It's not safe to cross the street.

4. Learning new vocabulary and making inferences often go hand in hand. Encourage your students to flip through a magazine or newspaper to find words they've never seen before or don't know the meanings of. Have each student write the sentences that contain these words on strips of paper. Put all the strips together and have students take turns drawing a sentence, reading it aloud, and using context clues to make an inference about a word's meaning. Have students look up the words in a dictionary to see how close the inference was to the actual meaning. You can even turn this activity into a game by dividing the class into teams and awarding a point for each correct inference a team makes.

Inferences

Goal: make inferences while reading

Sometimes we don't know exactly what's going on. Stories and conversations don't always include all the information we need to know right away what's happening. Often we have to make an inference, or a guess, about what's going on.

See if you can infer what's happening here.

> Corey squirmed in his seat. He could sense the tension all around. He closed his eyes as his little sister bounced the ball at the line. "Come on, Tanya," he thought. "You can do it." There was silence. Then the crowd exploded. Corey stood up and opened his eyes as the ball went through the hoop and the team ran over to hug his sister.

Here's a plan to help you make an inference.

- ◆ **Look for word clues.** The words you read will give you lots of hints.

    These words help you figure out what's going on in the story.
    - tense
    - bounced the ball
    - the crowd exploded
    - the ball went through the hoop

- ◆ **Think about what you already know.** Try to compare what's happening with experiences you've had in the past.

    For example, you know that when a team wins a close game, the crowd explodes!

- ◆ **Put yourself in the character's place.** Imagine you are the character. Pretend you are doing, seeing, hearing, and feeling everything the character is feeling.

- ◆ **Test your inference.** Once you think you know what is going on, reread the passage to see if your inference makes sense.

Inferences

Goal: Identify clues that support an inference

Each story below is followed by an inference about what is happening. Write the words or phrases that support the inference. An example is done for you.

1. Margo could barely stand still. There were only two people in front of her. Soon it would be her turn at the ticket window. Her dream was about to come true—to see her idol in person.

   Inference: Margo is buying tickets to see someone she admires.

   Clues: *barely stand still, dream, ticket window, idol, in person*

2. Uncle Jamal pushed his chair back from the table. "My, my, you have outdone yourself, Mom," he said. He patted his stomach and picked up his napkin. "I'm so full, I'm not sure I can get out of this chair."

   Inference: Uncle Jamal just ate a large, delicious meal.

   Clues: _____

3. "They're now entering the final lap. What a battle we've had out there today, folks. Number 24 still holds a slim lead, but it hasn't been easy. He survived a wreck all the way back on lap three. Now he's about to take the checkered flag for the first time in his young career."

   Inference: An announcer is describing the end of an auto race.

   Clues: _____

4. Zack looked at the sign again. It still said "Closed." He couldn't believe it. He really needed that book to finish his research report that was due tomorrow. Maybe the South Branch was still open. It wouldn't matter, though, because he didn't even know which bus route would take him there.

   Inference: Zack needs a book from the library but isn't able to get it.

   Clues: _____

Strategic Learning
Reading Comprehension: Level 2

Inferences

Goal: Use context clues to understand unfamiliar words

Making inferences can help you figure out the meaning of an unfamiliar word. Use context clues and what you already know to make an inference about the meaning of each word in italics.

1. After looking over the jellybeans in the jar for several minutes, Ian *surmised* there were well over one thousand.

   surmised means _____

2. After the speech, everyone talked about what a great *orator* Mr. Witherspoon is. He kept the audience interested for over an hour.

   orator means _____

3. "All he wants to do is sit in front of that computer," Ms. Rodriguez said. "He's turning into a real *technogeek*."

   technogeek means _____

4. Mr. Reed told us to use the proper *receptacle* instead of throwing our papers on the floor.

   receptacle means _____

5. I was *repulsed* by the smell of the rotten eggs.

   repulsed means _____

6. Why would you waste your money on such a *frivolous* thing? It's really just a piece of junk.

   frivolous means _____

7. Ben's teacher thought his excuse for late homework was such a *sham*, she gave him detention.

   sham means _____

8. Tim *evaded* the teacher's question about his research report by talking about the weather instead.

   evaded means _____

Inferences

Goal: Give reasons to support or refute inferences

Many times an inference that seems to make sense just isn't true. Each inference below contains one reason it might be true. Decide whether or not you agree with the inference. Then support or explain your decision.

1. More people would rather eat chocolate than broccoli, so chocolate must be better for us than broccoli.
   Do you agree or disagree with this inference? Why?

   _____

2. If a song is popular, then it must be a really good song.
   Do you agree or disagree with this inference? Why?

   _____

3. Soccer is the most popular sport in the world, except in the United States. That must mean that the people in America don't like soccer.
   Do you agree or disagree with this inference? Why?

   _____

4. Most doctors agree that exercise helps our hearts stay strong, so everyone should exercise.
   Do you agree or disagree with this inference? Why?

   _____

5. Computers are an important part of many businesses today. Everyone should become an expert at using a computer.
   Do you agree or disagree with this inference? Why?

   _____

6. Pit bulls often attack people, so no one should keep them as pets.
   Do you agree or disagree with this inference? Why?

   _____

Inferences

Goal: Make an inference to extend a story

Write a sentence that tells what you think happens next in each story.

1. Derek opened his bedroom door and the smell hit him. It wasn't really the odor of smoke he was used to, but it made him think that something was burning. He looked over at the computer and dropped his book bag.

2. The ball bounced around the rim and we both leaped for the rebound. My hands grabbed the ball over my head and I pulled it tight to my body. "Ow!" Amanda yelled. I looked over to see tears in her eyes and her hands over her mouth.

3. Ms. Carroll stood at the front of the room with her arms crossed. She narrowed her eyes and stared at each student, one by one. We all sat up straight in our desks. No one said a word. The corners of Ms. Carroll's mouth moved slightly. After minutes of silence, she finally opened her mouth.

4. Frank grabbed the wheel tightly as the pickup sped around him. It swerved back and forth on the road ahead. It looked like the driver was losing control. Frank looked in his rearview window, slowed down, and steered off the road.

Inferences

Goal: Use dialog to make inferences

Read what each person is saying. Then use the information to infer the speaker's occupation. Underline the words that helped you make your inference.

1. "I think we're about ready to go here. Let's get him numbed up. You might feel a little sting here, Danny."

   "There, I think that will do it."

   "I'll be back in just a few minutes, and we'll get that filling taken care of."

   What is this person's occupation? _____

2. "I can't believe what I'm seeing out there! Haven't any of you been paying attention?"

   "Robinson, you look like you're taking a walk through the park. Find your man and stick to him. He's lighting you up out there. And, Rodriguez, if you don't learn to take care of the ball better, you can sit on the bench with me."

   "Now let's get out there and make some good decisions this half!"

   What is this person's occupation? _____

3. "Hi. What can I do for you?"

   "Great. I might have something over here that you'll like. Looks like red might be your color. Why don't you just go in there and try it on? I'll see if I can find some other things you might like."

   What is this person's occupation? _____

4. "All right, order up. Here's your two over easy and wheat, no butter."

   "Could you guys write a little neater? How am I supposed to get these orders right if I can't read them?"

   "Would somebody grab me another box of bacon from the cooler? Looks like we have a table of 16 to do."

   What is this person's occupation? _____

Inferences

Goal: Make and revise inferences based on character information

The inferences we make often change as we receive more information. Read the story below and answer the questions. When you're finished, look at the inferences you made. How did they change as you learned more about the main character?

Maureen Lucas has always loved music. "When she was a baby, she would only be quiet while music played," her mom said. "It's the only way we could get her to settle down. And as she got older, she became even more active."

1. What words would you use to describe Maureen? Why?

_____

Today Maureen is a senior at Westside High. She plays flute in the concert band and also plays with the city orchestra. Her musical talents go beyond playing the flute, too. She taught herself to play guitar, plays the piano for the concert choir, and is a drummer for a local band. "I never thought about becoming a musician or what I would do when I got older," Maureen said. "It's just something that I've always done. Music is my life. Everything I do has something to do with music."

2. How would you describe Maureen now?

_____

3. Why do you think music is so important to her?

_____

"I'm not sure what Maureen would do if she didn't have music," her mom said. "She got very sick when she was three years old. She had a problem with her immune system. If she came in contact with other people, she caught diseases other people wouldn't.

"She couldn't leave the house most of the time, and it wasn't until she was in fifth grade that she could go to school with other kids. She spent all her time listening to music and playing music. Maureen couldn't stand sitting around watching TV and she didn't really enjoy reading. She was always too active to do those things. Luckily she discovered that music was something she could really focus on."

4. Now why do you think music is so important to Maureen?

_____

Inferences

Goal: Make inferences based on dialog

Read these conversations and answer the questions after each one.

"He's not going to sit with us, is he?" Marsha whispered.

"I hope not," Destiny answered. "He's supposed to just drop us off out front."

"What's all the whispering about back there?" Mr. Mack asked.

"Nothing, Dad," Destiny said. "Are we almost there? It starts at 8:00."

1. Where is this conversation taking place? _____
2. Where do you think they are going? _____
3. Why do you say that? _____

"This is the third time this month, Devan," Ms. Markowitz said.

"I know, I just keep forgetting," said Devan.

"Maybe we should try a new system. The assignment book doesn't seem to be working. Do you have any ideas?"

Devan said, "I don't know. Maybe I should write a note on the front of my book."

4. Where is this conversation taking place? _____
5. What do you think they are talking about? _____
6. Why do you say that? _____

"Excellent job, Kate," Dan said. "I can tell you've been working on this."

"I still mess up if I try to go too fast," Kate said. "My fingers just don't go where I want them to."

"We can work on that. I'm just glad you're getting all the notes correct," Dan said. "I think it's time we moved on to more challenging material, if you're ready."

Kate said, "I'll give it a try."

7. What is going on here? _____
8. How can you tell? _____

Strategic Learning
Reading Comprehension: Level 2

Inferences

Goal: Make inferences to complete dialogs

An important part of making inferences is putting yourself into the situation. Imagine you are involved in each dialog below. Read the entire dialog first. Try to determine what the setting is and what is happening. Then write what you would say on the blanks.

1. "Is there anything else I can get for you today?"

   _____

   _____

   "I'm sorry, I think we are all out of that. Is there another dessert I could get for you?"

   _____

   _____

   "Sorry about that. I'll just figure up your check then and be right back."

   _____

   _____

2. "Hey, this looks really good. Way to go! What did you do differently this time?"

   _____

   _____

   "It looks like you improved most in English. What did you do to get all that extra credit?"

   _____

   _____

   "Well, I think all your hard work deserves something special. After I sign this, we'll do something fun. Do you have any ideas?"

   _____

   _____

136
Copyright © 2002 LinguiSystems, Inc.

Strategic Learning
Reading Comprehension: Level 2

Inferences

Goal: Make inferences about a passage

Read this passage about the first astronauts to land on the moon.

In 1969, astronauts Neil Armstrong and Edwin Aldrin became the first human beings to set foot on the moon. The astronauts walked easily on the moon even though they were wearing heavy spacesuits. They felt light because the moon's gravity is six times weaker than Earth's gravity. A person who weighs 180 pounds on Earth weighs only 30 pounds on the moon.

Because there is so little gravity on the moon, there is also no atmosphere. That means the moon has no clouds, no rain, no wind, no water, and no air. The astronauts carried their own air with them so they could breathe. They had to talk to each other by radio because there was no air to carry sound.

While the astronauts were on the moon, they collected rocks and soil samples. They took a lot of pictures and set up some equipment to measure "moonquakes." The astronauts had no vehicles, so they didn't go far from where they landed.

Use the information you just read to answer these questions.

1. Armstrong and Aldrin left footprints in the moon's soil. Do you think those footprints are still there? Why?

   _____

   _____

2. Future astronauts brought an electric-powered car to the moon. Why did they do that?

   _____

   _____

3. If you weighed 120 pounds on Earth, how much would you weigh on the moon? Why?

   _____

   _____

4. What do you think a *moonquake* is?

   _____

   _____

Strategic Learning
Reading Comprehension: Level 2

Inferences

Goal: Make inferences based on titles

You can often tell a lot about something just by its title. Read these titles and answer the questions.

1. Movie title: *Zero Minutes to Destruction*
   Is this movie a comedy or a drama? Why?

   _____

2. Book title: *Rainy Day Guide to Beating Boredom*
   What do you think this book is about? Why?

   _____

3. TV Show: *Absolutely Incredible!*
   What's something you might expect to see on this show?

   _____

4. Internet Web site: *Your Father's Video Game Site*
   Does this sound like a site you would like to visit? Why?

   _____

5. Painting: *Paint Glob #16*
   Describe what you think this painting would look like.

   _____

6. CD title: *Wide-Open Spaces*
   What type of music do you think this is? Why?

   _____

7. Magazine: *Let's Get Going!*
   What kinds of articles would you find in this magazine?

   _____

Inferences

> Goal: Make inferences about a book

You make inferences every day, whenever you watch TV, read a book, or watch other people. Choose a book at random from the library. Follow the directions below and answer the questions.

Look at the title and cover of the book. Don't open it yet!

1. What is the title of the book? _____

2. Describe the cover of the book. _____
   _____
   _____
   _____

3. Do you think this book is fiction or nonfiction? Why?
   _____
   _____

Open the book and look at the first pages, including the table of contents (if there is one).

4. What do you think this book is about? Why?
   _____
   _____
   _____

Now read the first few pages of the book.

5. Do you think you will like this book? How can you tell?
   _____
   _____
   _____

Inferences

Goal: Make inferences to solve a mystery

Read this mystery and answer the questions about the inferences you made.

"So, the math test is missing?" Detective Findit asked, walking through the door.

"Yes," Ms. Karp answered, "and I don't have time to write another one. The students are in their seats ready to take it right now."

"When is the last time you saw the test?" the detective asked.

"Right before lunch. That's when I put it in this file cabinet."

"Has anyone else been in this room since you put it in there?" Detective Findit asked.

"I don't know. I ate my lunch at my desk and just left for a minute to take a phone call," Ms. Karp said. "When I came back from my phone call, I was going to get the test to make photocopies. I looked in the file cabinet and it had disappeared."

Detective Findit looked closely at the file cabinet and touched it. "What's this purple, sticky spot?"

"I have no idea," Ms. Karp said. "I've never noticed it before. Is it a clue?"

"It just might be," Detective Findit said. "The person who left this spot probably took your test." Then he looked at the class, "I'd like each person here who brought a lunch to come to the front of the room. I'll need to talk to each of you alone."

"I don't think that will be necessary," Ms. Karp said. She held one hand in the air, and her face was very red. She was looking at the math test. It was underneath the lunch bag on her desk.

1. Where does this story take place?

   _____

2. What time of day does it take place? How do you know?

   _____

3. What might the purple spot have been?

   _____

4. Why did Detective Findit want to talk to each student who had brought a lunch that day?

   _____

5. What do you think is the solution to this mystery?

   _____

Figurative Language

Instructor Information

> **Goal:** to understand, identify, and write figurative language
>
> **Objectives:** In this unit, your students will:
> - understand what figurative language is
> - identify and explain metaphors and similes
> - identify and explain idioms
> - identify and explain personification
> - identify and explain hyperbole
> - use metaphors, similes, idioms, personification, and hyperbole in writing tasks

To understand figurative language (metaphors, similes, idioms, personification, and hyperbole), students need to use their comparing and logical thinking skills. For reading success, it is important for students to identify and understand various forms of figurative language. When figurative language is used to describe something, students must be able to analyze and evaluate the information in order to comprehend what they are reading.

In this unit, students will understand and identify metaphors, similes, idioms, personification, and hyperbole. They will learn that metaphors and similes compare two items in different ways. They will learn that idioms mean something quite different from their literal meaning. They will learn that personification makes animals and objects come alive with meaning. They will also learn that hyperbole is a literary exaggeration. Once students can successfully identify figurative language, they will use what they have learned in writing tasks to demonstrate mastering these concepts.

Enrichment Activities

1. Create get-well cards for a sick classmate or teacher. Provide a starting phrase for the front of the cards and have students finish the phrase inside the cards. Have students work in pairs or individually. For example, "I was so sad to hear that you were sick that . . . ." on the front of the card and inside students might write "I cried a river of tears" or "I ate three banana splits." Have the students finish the project by illustrating their cards.

Figurative Language, continued

> Instructor Information

2. Poetry is a great source of figurative language. Bring in examples and/or have students bring in their favorite (or least favorite) poems. Analyze a poem as a class to get the students started. Then pair up the students and give each pair a poem to discuss and analyze. Have them write examples of figurative language and talk about what they think each one means or why the writer chose that wording.

3. Write thank-you cards to a class visitor or speaker to tell them how much you appreciated the person's visit. Make a list of starting phrases on the board, such as "Thank you for speaking to us. Your topic was like . . . ." or "Thank you for visiting our class. You made us feel like . . . ." Have each student choose a starting phrase for the front of his card and then write his own ending inside the card. For a humorous twist, students could illustrate the literal meanings rather than the figurative meanings for the expressions.

4. Have students watch commercials on TV or listen to them on the radio. Ask students to jot down examples and label the types of figurative language they hear. Share observations and compare notes as a class. Talk about how figurative language in advertising helps sell the products.

5. Cut out examples of figurative language from magazines and newspapers. Write the various types of figurative language on slips of paper and place them in a container. Have students help make a montage on the bulletin board by posting the figurative language examples along with their labels.

6. The sports section of a local newspaper is usually a good place to find idioms (e.g., *hit the boards, swept the series, broke the record, make the cut*). Have your students use non-figurative language to rewrite the sentences with idioms. Compare the two pieces of writing. Which one is more interesting to read? Why?

7. Provide students with a list of idioms. Have each student pick one of the idioms and draw a picture of the literal meaning of the idiom. Then have the students write what the idioms really mean below their pictures. Have your students exchange papers and take turns guessing the idiom the other student has illustrated.

8. Write a list of hyperboles on the board or provide them on a handout. Assign each student a different example. Have the students illustrate the exaggerated expressions and then exchange their papers. Ask the students to match the literal drawings to the hyperboles they illustrate and then talk about the meaning behind each hyperbole.

Figurative Language

Goal: learn about different kinds of figurative language

Do you <u>get cold feet</u> whenever you have a writing assignment? ← idiom <u>Is your writing a sleep potion?</u> ← hyperbole If you used figurative language, you could be <u>the greatest writer in the world</u>. ← metaphor Your <u>words would sing, dance, and leap off the page</u>. ← personification After all, <u>a story without figurative language is like an Oreo cookie without the white stuff</u>! ← simile

The paragraph above is loaded with different types of figurative language that you can use in your writing. Here's a description of each type.

◆ **idiom** a phrase or expression that says one thing but means something entirely different

I'm in a lather about this pimple on my nose.

◆ **metaphor** a comparison of two unlike things that says one thing is actually something else. Metaphors use the words *is*, *are*, *was*, and *were*.

The pimple on my nose is a volcano ready to erupt.

◆ **hyperbole** an exaggerated expression that makes characters or situations much bigger or smaller than they really are

You can see the pimple on my nose halfway around the world!

◆ **personification** giving human characteristics to animals or objects

The pimple on my nose is screaming for everyone's attention.

◆ **simile** uses the words *like* or *as* to compare people, objects, or events

The pimple on my nose is like a volcano ready to explode.

Strategic Learning
Reading Comprehension: Level 2

Figurative Language

Goal: Choose the correct simile or metaphor

Choose a simile or metaphor from the box that best fits each sentence. Then decide whether it is a simile or metaphor. In the blank in front of each sentence, write an **S** for *simile* or an **M** for *metaphor*.

a rocket	an animal
an oven	as hard as a rock
like an egg	as gentle as a lamb
a jungle	as fast as the wind
a tank	like a stone

1. _____ The runner was _____. He broke the world record.

2. _____ Her third pitch was _____. The batter didn't have a chance.

3. _____ That vase is _____. If you drop it, it will break.

4. _____ Tasha is the nicest person I know. She's _____.

5. _____ Look at the size of Tracy's car. What _____!

6. _____ Don't eat that stale cookie. It's _____.

7. _____ The front yard is _____. I haven't mowed it in three weeks.

8. _____ Dwayne is _____ in football games. No one can stop him.

9. _____ With the furnace blasting, this movie theater is _____.

10. _____ When Eli gets into a pool, he sinks _____.

144
Copyright © 2002 LinguiSystems, Inc.

Strategic Learning
Reading Comprehension: Level 2

Figurative Language

Goal: Identify and explain similes and metaphors

Underline the simile or metaphor in each sentence. Then write its meaning on the line.

1. "Chan!" his aunt yelled. "Your room is a pigsty."

   _____

2. "You need to work until it's as clean as a whistle."

   _____

3. Chan sighed. He liked to clean about as much as getting his teeth pulled.

   _____

4. Chan began to sort through his clothes. They were piled in a heap as tall as a mountain.

   _____

5. When he changed his sheets, he found some socks that smelled like a skunk.

   _____

6. Then Chan discovered some pizza under his bed. It must have been there a while because it was a triangle of cement.

   _____

7. When Chan was finished cleaning, his aunt praised him for all his hard work. She didn't notice his closet. It was as full as a hibernating bear.

   _____

Strategic Learning
Reading Comprehension: Level 2

Figurative Language

Goal: Choose the correct idiom

Choose an idiom from the box to complete each sentence.

1. James didn't want to stay for the ceremony, so he

   _____.

2. Everyone was watching Adam instead of listening to the

   concert. He really _____.

3. We have to _____ if we want

   to finish our project on time.

4. Thanks for the jacket you gave me. It fits me

   _____.

5. This math assignment is hard. I can't _____.

6. I'm angry that I can't go to the movie tonight. It really _____.

7. I can't wait to go to the skating party next week! We will _____.

8. Jana isn't sure she wants to buy your CD player. Let her _____

   and she'll let you know tomorrow.

9. What are you thinking about? I'll give you a _____.

10. It's your responsibility to walk the dog, not mine. Don't _____.

pass the buck
stole the spotlight
like a glove
sleep on it
have a ball
make heads or tails of it
keep the ball rolling
burns me up
flew the coop
penny for your thoughts

146
Copyright © 2002 LinguiSystems, Inc.

Strategic Learning
Reading Comprehension: Level 2

Figurative Language

Goal: Identify and explain idioms

Underline the idiom in each sentence. Then write what it means.

1. The new Grisly Girls' CD is so great, it will knock your socks off.
   _____

2. I don't want to get into a big fight, so let's nip this thing in the bud.
   _____

3. If we plan the party carefully, everything will go like clockwork.
   _____

4. "Don't get so upset, Bridget," Ryan laughed. "I was just pulling your leg."
   _____

5. You can't tell Rosemary any secrets because she spills the beans every time.
   _____

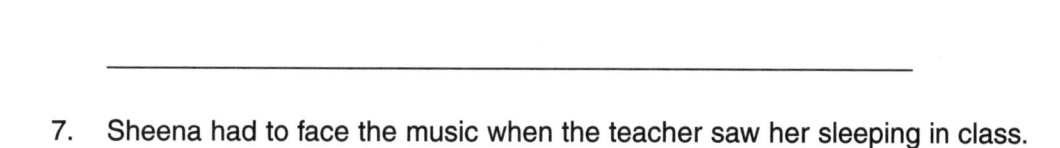

6. I was so tired, I was out like a light as soon as I got under the covers.
   _____

7. Sheena had to face the music when the teacher saw her sleeping in class.
   _____

8. You're barking up the wrong tree if you think I'm going to play a practical joke on the principal.
   _____

9. Anjie blew her stack when she saw her dog tearing up her assignment.
   _____

10. Instead of telling the truth right away, Jennifer beat around the bush.
    _____

Figurative Language

Goal: Explain idioms in context

Idioms are figurative expressions that don't mean exactly what the words say.

Boy, I really **struck out** when I asked for an extension on my science project.

Read what this deejay has to say and underline each idiom she uses. Then write what each idiom means.

1. Suzy Kincaid here with the latest K-ROX weather. Sorry, it looks like it's going to rain cats and dogs.

   _____

2. I won't pull the wool over your eyes, I'll just tell you we're going to have bad weather.

   _____

3. Enough about weather, let's get back on track with some music.

   _____

4. Let's blast off with the top hits of the 70s, including "Another One Bites the Dust."

   _____

5. Well, I'm not quite ready to bite the dust, but my time is up.

   _____

6. Stay cool, and I'll talk to you tomorrow.

   _____

148
Copyright © 2002 LinguiSystems, Inc.

Strategic Learning
Reading Comprehension: Level 2

Figurative Language

> Goal: Choose the best explanation of personification

Writers use personification to make their writing more interesting and to make it come alive. Circle the best explanation for the personification in each sentence below.

1. "Jason finally spotted the basketball shoes he'd been searching for. They were begging to be worn."

    The writer wants you to know that _____.

    a. shoes can talk

    b. the shoes were perfect for Jason in every way

    c. the shoes were Jason's size

2. "The stream laughed as it tumbled over the rocks."

    The writer wants to give the feeling that _____.

    a. the stream was very happy

    b. the stream was alive

    c. the water was flowing in an upbeat and lighthearted way

3. "The suitcase opened its mouth and swallowed the clothes."

    The writer wants you to picture _____.

    a. a mean, hungry suitcase

    b. someone shutting a suitcase with a lot of clothes inside

    c. something that wouldn't ever happen

4. "The night wind knocked on my window and tried to get in."

    The writer is suggesting that _____.

    a. the wind is blowing hard

    b. the wind has knuckles

    c. the wind sounds scary

5. "The old lion smirked royally, looking down his nose at us."

    The writer wants us to think that _____.

    a. the lion looked very regal, like a king

    b. the lion smiled and wore a crown

    c. the lion thought he was better than we are

Strategic Learning
Reading Comprehension: Level 2

Figurative Language

Goal: Identify and explain personification

Underline the personification in each sentence. Then write its true meaning on the line.

1. My blank computer screen glared at me as I tried to write my report.
   _____

2. The grass tickled the baby's feet.
   _____

3. The waves roared onto the beach.
   _____

4. The sun came out and chased the rain away.
   _____

5. During the snowstorm, the wind screamed around the corner of the school.
   _____

6. The flower wilted sadly. No one had remembered to water it.
   _____

7. The new spring leaves twisted with joy in the gentle breeze.
   _____

8. The haunted house screeched at the girl as she opened its front door.
   _____

9. The iron spit and hissed as it ran up and down the shirt.
   _____

10. The clothes on the clothesline danced in the wind.
    _____

Figurative Language

Goal: Choose the correct meanings for hyperbole examples

Circle the correct meaning for each hyperbole.

1. Even a dictionary would have failed that spelling test.

    a. The spelling words weren't in the dictionary.

    b. The teacher must have made up all the words.

    c. The test was extremely difficult.

2. Dana is faster than a speeding bullet.

    a. Dana can run really fast.

    b. Dana is Superwoman.

    c. Bullets aren't really that fast.

3. Mr. Wyatt's dog is bigger and meaner than a mother grizzly bear protecting her cubs.

    a. The dog is going to have puppies.

    b. The dog is big and wooly.

    c. You should stay far away from the dog.

4. Jared's mom took his clothes into his room. It'll take her all day just to find his closet.

    a. Jared's room is really messy.

    b. Jared's mom gets mixed up easily.

    c. Jared's room is as big as a castle.

5. When Lisa sneezed, she blew out the windows in the apartment next door.

    a. The windows were extremely fragile.

    b. Lisa's sneeze was really loud.

    c. The neighbor fell through the window when he heard the sneeze.

Strategic Learning
Reading Comprehension: Level 2

Figurative Language

Goal: Identify and explain hyperbole

Underline the hyperbole in each sentence. Then write its true meaning on the line.

1. Daniel cried a river of tears.
   _____

2. For the hundredth time, pick up your clothes.
   _____

3. The phone in the office was ringing off the hook.
   _____

4. My camping backpack weighs a ton.
   _____

5. It's so hot today, you could cook an egg on the sidewalk.
   _____

6. It's so quiet in class, you could hear a pin drop.
   _____

7. It's going to take me a year to finish my drawing.
   _____

8. I ate so many tacos, I could explode.
   _____

9. Finding my friend at the mall was like trying to find a needle in a haystack.
   _____

10. The crack in the basement wall was the size of the Grand Canyon.
    _____

152
Copyright © 2002 LinguiSystems, Inc.

Strategic Learning
Reading Comprehension: Level 2

Figurative Language

Goal: Recognize and label figurative language in a passage

| simile | metaphor | idiom | hyperbole | personification |

Underline the example of figurative language in each sentence and write its name on the line. Then take turns explaining the meaning of each sentence with a partner.

1. _____ Mr. Henkle is a stick of dynamite waiting to go off.

2. _____ Lisa's singing voice is as sweet as cotton candy.

3. _____ Listening to that lecture was like having my fingernails yanked out.

4. _____ The walls of the old house moaned and shuddered in the hurricane.

5. _____ Jamal's legs were so long, he could step over the Mississippi River.

6. _____ Mike needs to cut to the chase and say what's really going on.

7. _____ The old dog lay down as if to say, "YOU go fetch the stick!"

8. _____ Ian's birthday gift money was burning a hole in his pocket.

Strategic Learning
Reading Comprehension: Level 2

153

Copyright © 2002 LinguiSystems, Inc.

Figurative Language

Goal: Recognize and label figurative language in a passage

Read the newspaper article. Underline any examples of figurative language you find in the article. Label each example with the appropriate letter from the box on the right.

simile = **S**
metaphor = **M**
idiom = **I**
hyperbole = **H**
personification = **P**

The Rockets Take Off!

The Fairfield Rockets were true to their name last night. They blasted off early in the first quarter and didn't slow down until the final buzzer in the fourth. Becker was a monster out there on the court and Evans was a fiery locomotive. Neither forward could be stopped. These two lit up the scoreboard with 54 points. In fact, the Rockets scored so many points that the scoreboard shorted out trying to keep up!

Even when the score was 98-32 in the second half, the Pistons didn't throw in the towel. The Rockets were just too hot to handle. The best play of the game came in the fourth quarter. Stokes stole the ball and, as quick as lightning, fed the ball to Becker, who soared like an eagle, dunking the ball to make the score 87-23. The writing was on the wall. The Rockets were going to win and win big. Even the ball got into the game, giving a little cheer each time it slipped through the net. The final score was 115-45, Rockets soaring over the Pistons.

"It was a team win," Becker said after the game. "We were all hitting the boards pretty hard tonight. It was sweet!"

Figurative Language

Goal: Use figurative language in sentences

Make these sentences more interesting by rewriting them with figurative language. Choose from idioms, personification, metaphors, similes, or hyperbole.

1. My sister takes a really long time to get ready for school every morning.

   _____

2. I am really hungry.

   _____

3. Dion's teacher talked very fast.

   _____

4. It was hot in the school bus.

   _____

Choose at least three different types of figurative language. Write your own sentences. Put more than one type of figurative language in the same sentence, if you dare!

5. _____

6. _____

7. _____

8. _____

Strategic Learning
Reading Comprehension: Level 2

Imagery

Instructor Information

Goal: to understand and use sensory information in a variety of reading passages

Objectives: In this unit, your students will:

- understand imagery
- identify and use describing words and phrases
- identify and use sensory words
- use metaphors and similes to describe
- apply knowledge of imagery to a variety of reading and writing tasks

To successfully understand information in some reading passages, students need to form sharp mental images of what they are reading. These images help students understand and remember what they are reading. The words become more vivid by exciting the senses and creating richer meaning and association pathways in the brain. As writers, students need to use descriptive words and phrases in order to help their readers appreciate the information in what the writers have written.

In this unit, students will understand how imagery can help them better comprehend what they are reading. Then they will identify and use describing words, sensory words, metaphors, and similes in a variety of writing tasks.

Enrichment Activities

1. Have students search magazine and newspaper advertisements for vivid descriptions and describing words. Have them cut out the words and phrases and post them on a class bulletin board. Talk about how the words help the reader visualize the message. Discuss why advertisers use these vivid descriptions for their products.

2. Have students choose favorite characters from literature and write descriptions of these characters. Encourage students to appeal to all the senses as they describe their characters. Explain that they are describing the characters for someone who has never read the stories. Have students exchange their descriptions and mark the sensory details used in the descriptions.

Imagery, continued | Instructor Information

3. Lead a discussion to help your students determine which types of entertainment allow us to visualize, which forms do the visualizing for us, and which ones are a combination. For example, video games aren't like real life, so although we can see the action, we often visualize ourselves taking a part in the action. Here are some other forms of entertainment to discuss:

   symphony concert
   music CD
   pop music concert
   TV show
   music on radio
   sporting event on radio
   magazine
   novel
   movie

4. Figurative language is one tool a writer uses to help the reader visualize. A simile is a common device most writers use, but one that students sometimes find difficult to grasp. Introduce the idea of similes to your more concrete learners by having them correct illogical similes. Write illogical similes such as the ones below and ask your students to correct them.

   quick like a snail
   as lovely as a pile of mud
   bright as a burned-out light bulb
   as dark as daybreak

   Encourage your students to compose some of their own illogical similes for their classmates to correct.

5. Play a piece of classical music for your students. Be sure to choose a selection that will evoke a sense of place or action. Recordings of Mozart's "Salzburg Symphonies" or Beethoven's "Pastoral Symphony (No. 6, first movement)" are readily available and will easily stir your students' visualizing skills. As they listen to the piece, encourage them to draw pictures that represent what their minds are "seeing" or have students make a list of describing words or phrases that represent how the music makes them feel. When the piece is over, have students share what they've written or drawn. Did everyone "see" the same thing?

Imagery

> Goal: Understand and use imagery to form clear mental images

When you read, you form ideas in your mind of the things you're reading about. Words or phrases that are colorful or appeal to your five senses help you understand and remember what you read. These interesting words or phrases are called **imagery** because they help you imagine.

What images do you get in your mind as you read this passage?

> My grandmother is 85 years old and I don't think she has ever thrown a single thing away. It's a good thing she lives alone because there is only room for one person to walk around in her apartment. A single, narrow path winds through the place. It is stacked on all sides with piles of books, newspapers, and magazines. There are also shoeboxes full of photos and postcards stacked like Lego blocks. Grandma says she loves to be there surrounded by all her "treasures." She doesn't hear the constant hum of her refrigerator. She doesn't smell kitty litter that hasn't been changed for days. She's as happy as a cat on a sunny windowsill. Grandma always has good stories to tell. Visiting her is like reading a great book!

A good writer writes so the reader can picture what was in his mind as he wrote. Here's a plan to help you visualize what you read.

- ◆ **Look for descriptive words and phrases.**
  - 85 years old
  - A single, narrow path winds through the place.

- ◆ **Look for words that appeal to the five senses.**
  - the constant hum of her refrigerator
  - kitty litter that hasn't been changed for days

- ◆ **Look for metaphors and similes.**
  - postcards stacked like Lego blocks
  - as happy as a cat on a sunny windowsill

Imagery

Goal: Identify and use descriptive words and phrases

Certain kinds of words can help you understand what you read about very clearly. These descriptive words or phrases are **imagery**. They give you a clear mental image of something by telling you what it looks, smells, sounds, tastes, or feels like.

Underline the words and phrases that help you understand what the event below was like.

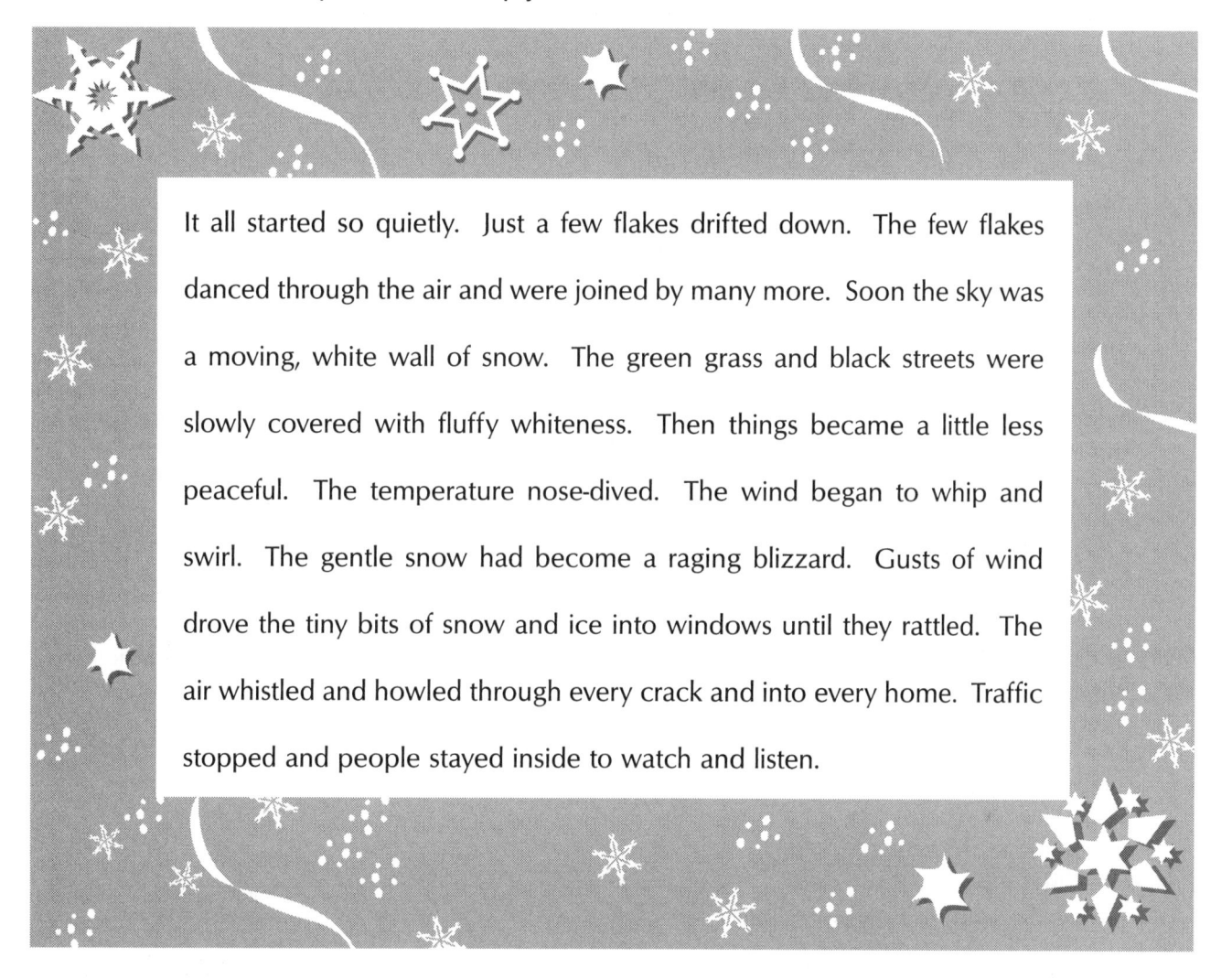

It all started so quietly. Just a few flakes drifted down. The few flakes danced through the air and were joined by many more. Soon the sky was a moving, white wall of snow. The green grass and black streets were slowly covered with fluffy whiteness. Then things became a little less peaceful. The temperature nose-dived. The wind began to whip and swirl. The gentle snow had become a raging blizzard. Gusts of wind drove the tiny bits of snow and ice into windows until they rattled. The air whistled and howled through every crack and into every home. Traffic stopped and people stayed inside to watch and listen.

Now write a short paragraph on a separate sheet of paper using descriptive words. Describe one of the following:

an interesting person you know

an unusual place you've visited

something strange that belongs to you

a time when you were very happy

Imagery

Goal: Identify sensory details in context

A writer uses descriptive words and phrases to help you create a clear mental picture of a character. Good descriptions use details that appeal to a reader's senses. Read this character description and follow the directions.

The creature was like nothing I had ever seen. It stood well over ten feet tall with one large, curly horn sticking up from its head. A long, thick tail dragged behind the monster as it walked. I felt the ground tremble as it came closer. The creature's arms hung nearly to the ground. Instead of fingers on its hand, it had two foot-long claws. The creature's odor was its most frightening feature, though. It smelled like a mixture of rotten eggs and wet, dirty fur.

I licked my lips and moved backward. The inside of my mouth tasted like something metal. I think that was the taste of fear.

The creature's tiny green eyes stared at me while its tooth-filled mouth opened wide. It roared and created a sound no human had probably ever heard.

What sensory details does the writer include in this description? Write a sensory detail the writer used to appeal to each sense below.

1. sight _____

2. hearing _____

3. touch _____

4. smell _____

5. taste _____

Imagery

Goal: Provide sensory details

Look at each picture. Write details that would appeal to the senses listed. Then use your list to write a descriptive paragraph on another sheet of paper. Write your description so that your reader can clearly picture the item.

sight _____

taste _____

smell _____

touch _____

sound _____

◇◇◇◇◇◇◇◇◇◇◇◇◇◇◇◇◇◇◇◇◇◇

sight _____

taste _____

smell _____

touch _____

sound _____

Strategic Learning
Reading Comprehension: Level 2

Imagery

Goal: identify and use descriptive words and phrases

The descriptive words and phrases in this paragraph give you a clear mental image of the monster Frankenstein.

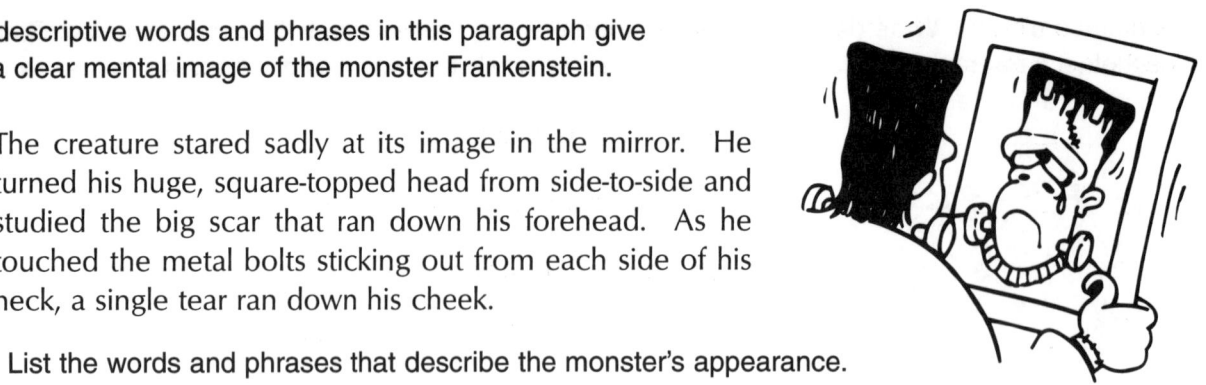

> The creature stared sadly at its image in the mirror. He turned his huge, square-topped head from side-to-side and studied the big scar that ran down his forehead. As he touched the metal bolts sticking out from each side of his neck, a single tear ran down his cheek.

1. List the words and phrases that describe the monster's appearance.

   _____

   _____

2. List the words and phrases that show the monster's feelings.

   _____

   _____

Now write a short paragraph describing each of these two people. Use descriptive words or phrases to bring each character to life.

_____   _____

_____   _____

_____   _____

_____   _____

162
Copyright © 2002 LinguiSystems, Inc.

Strategic Learning
Reading Comprehension: Level 2

Imagery

Goal: Identify and use sensory words

Underline the words in the following sentences that help you imagine what is being described. Then write whether each sentence appeals to your sense of smell, sight, sound, taste, or touch.

1. _____ The door to the old house creaked noisily as it slowly swung open.

2. _____ As Kendra stepped through the doorway, she pushed away sticky cobwebs that grabbed at her from all directions.

3. _____ The old, vacant house smelled dusty and damp.

4. _____ Kendra shuddered when she heard a mouse scurry across the floor.

5. _____ She was staring at the ghostly shapes of sheet-covered furniture when a hand grabbed her shoulder.

6. _____ Kendra screamed like a frightened hyena.

7. _____ "Calm down," said Jess, glancing around nervously. "It's just me. I found our ball."

"Great!" said Kendra, sighing with relief. "Let's get out of this creepy place!"

Now read the following description and imagine the scene. Add sensory words to bring the scene to life. Then share your version of the scene with a partner to compare your imagery.

Royal groaned _____ as he looked at the _____ mess around him. There were _____ eggs on the floor and _____ milk on the _____ counter. _____ flour dust covered everything, including Royal. Well, at least he would soon have some of those _____ cookies to eat. Suddenly Royal realized there was a _____ smell coming from the oven. When he _____ opened the oven door, _____ smoke poured out _____. Royals' cookies looked like _____.

Strategic Learning
Reading Comprehension: Level 2

Imagery

Goal: Recognize how imagery affects the reader's feelings

How many times have you read something that made you feel sad, happy, or frightened? A writer who uses imagery well can create scenes that will make you feel different ways. Read each sentence below and choose a word from the box that names the emotion a reader might feel.

> relief   boredom   celebration   fear   revenge

1. As I stood in the middle of the damp basement, the lights all went out. All I could hear was scratching and squeaking sounds coming from the corner.   _____

2. My two days of worrying melted away in a second when the teacher handed me my test.   _____

3. Keith's eyelids began to droop and his head sagged as his teacher's voice droned on and on.   _____

4. "No one takes a cupcake from my lunch and gets away with it," he growled. "I'll get him back for this."   _____

5. Delia's arms shot into the air as she crossed the finish line a step ahead of the next runner.   _____

Now picture things in your mind that make you feel each emotion below. Write a sentence that describes each feeling or describes the situation in which you'd have each feeling.

6. sadness _____
   _____

7. jealousy _____
   _____

8. indifference _____
   _____

9. protectiveness _____
   _____

Imagery

Goal: Identify imagery

The passage below contains imagery that appeals to the senses. Underline the imagery.

Laura shifted in her chair uneasily. She forced her eyes to stay open. An unexpected yawn made her eyes water. The speaker's boring voice droned on and on, slower and slower, wrapping Laura's ears with soothing, velvet sounds. The warmth of the room seemed to melt her arms and legs into cooked noodles. Laura longed to put her head down and sleep the day away.

Glancing around slowly like an ancient turtle, Laura noticed that several students were struggling to stay awake, some unsuccessfully. Soft snoring reached her drowsy ears. She momentarily rested her head on her arm. Laura's nostrils breathed in the scent of pencil erasers, notebooks, and students after PE on a warm day.

Soon Laura's thoughts began to drift away. Her eyelids groaned under their own weight. Before she knew it, Laura had slumped down in her seat and was fast asleep.

Moments later, Laura's body grew restless. Still in a sleep trance, she raised her heavy head from her desk. Her head and one arm fell back and her mouth gaped open like a cave. Laura's papers rustled to the floor as a giant snore escaped from her. She didn't even hear the weak clapping that signaled the end of the speaker's talk.

Imagery

Goal: Identify imagery

The passage below contains imagery that appeals to the senses. Underline the imagery.

Michael's dark eyes squinted tightly as he walked toward his sister. Anger gripped his body, making his legs stiff and his back ramrod straight. His little sister, Nikki, sat in front of the TV, oblivious to the world around her.

Michael grabbed Nikki's shoulder, sensing the thin, delicate bones hidden beneath her sweater. Surprised, Nikki sucked in her breath and stared at Michael with wide eyes. Michael pushed his face close to hers. He was so close, he could smell peanut butter on her breath and count each freckle on her tiny nose. He noticed she had a small scab on her tiny chin. "She probably fell off her fancy new bike," Michael thought.

"Hey, did you touch my radio?" Michael demanded. Not waiting for an answer, he plowed on like a runaway freight train barreling down a mountain track. "Don't you ever touch any of my stuff again, you got that?" he yelled.

Nikki's soft brown eyes pooled with salty tears. Michael's stomach did flip-flops and his heart melted with understanding. Nikki was only six. "Sorry, Nikki," he said. "I'm just having a bad day. Let's go outside and ride bikes. You take the lead and set the pace." Nikki beamed from ear-to-ear as they headed for the garage.

Answer Key

Wherever these answers are given as sample responses, accept other logical, appropriate responses as correct.

Main Idea

Page 10
1. b
2. c
3. b

Page 11
1. b
2. c
3. c
4. a

Page 12
1. c
2. a
3. b

Page 13
1. a, c, d
2. b, c, e
3. a, b, e
4. a, b, e

Page 14
1. Sloth bears are <u>very active</u> and <u>very brave</u>, too. They <u>climb trees to gather honey right from the beehive</u>. Their <u>long, shaggy fur looks messy</u>, but the <u>cubs can easily hang from their mothers' backs while they travel</u> around the forest.
2. When it gets cold out, animals stay warm in different ways. Some animals <u>go to warmer areas</u>. Some animals just <u>go to sleep until spring</u>. Other animals <u>fluff up their fur or feathers</u>. Some small animals, like bees, <u>huddle into a tight ball to keep each other warm</u>.
3. Fireworks have <u>two kinds of gunpowder</u>. The powder is <u>packed into a paper tube called a rocket</u>. When you light the <u>fuse, one kind of gunpowder starts to burn</u>. This <u>makes the rocket go up</u>. When the rocket is high in the sky, <u>the heat sets fire to the rest of the gunpowder</u>. <u>The rocket explodes, creating colorful designs in the sky.</u>
4. Space Camp is for anyone who wants to be an astronaut. Campers stay for five days. They <u>hear lectures, watch films, tour a space flight center, and launch model rockets</u>. The best part is a <u>simulated space shuttle mission</u>. <u>They launch the shuttle, fix a satellite, and land.</u> Space Camp is a great way to learn about space travel.

Page 15
1. It's a <u>scooter</u>! It's a <u>skateboard</u>! <u>Take off the handle and the Scoot-n-Skate is a skateboard.</u> <u>Put the handle back on and you've got a scooter.</u> It's <u>easy to use</u> and it <u>comes in lots of colors</u>.

   Get the Scoot-n-Skate today!

   It's <u>2 toys in 1</u>!
   Main Idea: c
2. What do books, computers, and fun have in common? You can find them all at the Dayton Public Library. We get <u>new books weekly</u>. We have <u>monthly reading contests</u>, too! And you can <u>play the latest games on our computers</u>. We know you'll have fun at the library!
   Main Idea: a
3. Got cold feet? Then you'll love our <u>battery-operated</u> warming socks. These *cozy* socks will <u>keep your toes warm, even on the coldest days</u>. Just <u>one AAA battery in each sock</u> will <u>keep your feet warm</u> for <u>up to 24 hours</u>. Only <u>$12.95</u>. <u>One size fits most</u>. <u>Call now and you'll get an extra pair free!</u> And don't forget to <u>ask about our hats and mittens</u>!
   Main Idea: c

Page 16
1. Main Idea: Hogans
   underline (any 3): good for desert living, mound-like buildings made from mud and logs, mud walls keep hogans cool in summer and warm in winter, did not have windows, one door faced east, hole in the roof
2. Main Idea: Tepees
   underline (any 3): put up and take down in a hurry, cone-shaped tents, tied long wooden poles together at top, spread out bottom of poles, stretched animal hides over poles, painted pictures on the outside, fire in center, small hole in top

Page 17
1. Main Idea: Black widow spiders are deadly.
   Underline: bite is very painful, feel bad within an hour, bad headache, sick to your stomach, muscles may go into spasms, could die
2. Main Idea: how mosquitoes choose the people they bite
   Underline: soft moist skin, carbon dioxide in your breath, chemicals in your sweat, lactic acid in your body

Strategic Learning
Reading Comprehension: Level 2

167

Copyright © 2002 LinguiSystems, Inc.

Answer Key, continued

3. Main Idea: Roaches are pests, but they are good for medical research.
   Underline: used to study heart disease, used for cancer research, used to learn things about the human brain

Page 18

1. If everyone helped, <u>we could clean up the litter around our school in less than an hour</u>. Then our school would look much better. We could bring big garbage bags. ~~There are some in the supply room.~~ We could pick up the trash, bag it, and throw it in the dumpster. ~~The dumpster is never full because it is emptied twice a week.~~

2. <u>There was a break-in last week at Hayes Elementary School.</u> ~~My cousin is in fifth grade there.~~ The vandals got in through a window. At least ten computers, two VCRs, and nine TVs were stolen. Paint was smeared down a hallway. ~~The hallway leads to the gym.~~ Police have no suspects yet.

3. <u>The Knox County Sheriff's Department has lost a best friend</u>, a German shepherd police dog named Rex. Rex died from a virus earlier this month. Rex had been helping officers for over ten years. He was trained to sniff out drugs. ~~He liked to eat hot dogs.~~ A new dog named Jake has replaced Rex. ~~Jake was trained at the same place Rex was.~~

4. <u>Part of an amusement park ride collapsed on Tuesday.</u> A steel tower that supports a slingshot ride crashed to the ground at Smoky Point Amusement Park. No one was near the tower when it snapped. ~~The park is closed for the winter.~~ The cause has not been determined. There were no strong winds at the time. ~~The park will open again on May 25th.~~

Sequencing

Page 22
time words: today, after, first, then, at eleven o'clock, then, before
sequence: e, a, d, c, b

Page 23
1925—Picture sent to TV screen
1930—NBC started first TV station
1954—Color TV nationwide
1956—WNBQ first all-color station
1965—90% U.S. homes have TVs
2002—At least two TVs in most U.S. homes

Page 24
1889—Movie camera invented
1895—First movie shown in Paris
1903—First movie made and shown in the U.S.
1927—Sound added to movies
Today—Movie rental and purchase available, can go to cinemas

Page 25
1869—Born; taught to respect life
1882—Married
1891—Finished law school
1893—Moved to South Africa; worked for Indians' rights
1915—Returned to India; taught nonviolent protest of unfair laws
1920—Great leader and teacher
1948—Shot and killed

Page 26
1845—Telegraph invented
1876—Telephone invented
1906—First radio via airwaves
1936—TV with sound and pictures
1962—First satellite communication
1980s—Cell phone and fax invented
1990s—Internet around the world
2000—video telephone invented

Page 27
put your name on the paper
answer the questions you know
go back to the ones you skipped
check your answers

You breathe carbon dioxide into the air.
Plants use carbon dioxide to make food.
Plants send oxygen into the air.
We breathe the oxygen.

Page 28
You dial a phone number.
An electric signal travels to a central phone switch.
The switch sends the call to another switch.
The call is sent to the number you dialed.
Digital switches carry your voice over the wires as electrical impulses.

Page 29
1950s—first rock 'n' roll hit
1956—Elvis Presley recorded "Heartbreak Hotel."
1962—Beatles
late 1960s—Woodstock concert
1970s—Disco and punk rock
1981—Rock music videos on MTV
1985—Live Aid concert in July
Timeline:
12/7/41—Pearl Harbor attack; JFK applied for Navy sea duty
late 1942—assigned to boat squadron
8/2/43—PT boat destroyed
8/7/43—Crew rescued
Flowchart:
Became PT boat commander
With injured back, led PT crew after boat destroyed by Japanese
Pulled crewman ashore
Searched four days for help; got natives to get help
Awarded medals for heroism,

168
Copyright © 2002 LinguiSystems, Inc.

Strategic Learning
Reading Comprehension: Level 2

Answer Key, continued

leadership, and being wounded in combat

Page 30
Answers will vary.

Page 31
1. butterfly
2. top-to-bottom, side-to-side, front-to-back

Answers will vary.

Page 32
1. Statue of Liberty
2. Answers will vary.

Context Clues

Page 37
1. a
2. a
3. b
4. a
5. b
6. b
7. a

Page 38
1. pilots with another pilot
2. the act of graduating
3. two times a year
4. not persuasive
5. to turn into a liquid
6. able to be irritated
7. able to be compared
8. to take down from the throne

Page 39
1. big, bite, nibble; front teeth
2. pilot, fly; pilot
3. like a waterfall down the back of its head; fall like a waterfall
4. produce their seeds in cones, like pine trees; trees with pine cones
5. desert, dry, water; save, keep
6. no particles in the air; space without anything in it
7. remains of living things, rock, fossils; protected, made lasting

Page 40
1. speed, swiftness
2. make up
3. refinishing, renewing
4. clear, able to see through
5. extra pieces to complete outfits

Page 41
1. confused
2. sickening, gross
3. pep, energy
4. argument
5. touchy, particular

Page 42
1. eat, consume
2. building
3. fall apart, break into pieces
4. unreal picture
5. tiny models

Page 43
1. excited, very eager
2. large quantity/amount
3. choices of food dishes
4. creation
5. tomato

Page 44
1. predicament
2. hoax
3. optimistic
4. utensils
5. apathetic
6. digressed
7. quorum
8. cavalier
9. scaffold
10. receptionist

Page 45
1. pupils
2. enthusiasm
3. grant
4. restrained
5. judicial
6. fields
7. inquiries
8. engagement
9. gratitude

Page 46
Words and meanings will vary.

Page 47
1. c
2. b
3. d

Predicting

Pages 51-61
Predictions will vary.

Cause and Effect

Page 65
1. a, c; like school vacations, like kids
2. b, c; to learn about new jobs, to have fun
3. a, c; believe in its mission
4. a, b; to promote a cause or an action
5. b, c; doesn't like red meat
6. b, c; to make good money
7. a, c; to meet new people
8. a, b; to tone up, to start playing a sport

Page 66
1. buildings destroyed, trees pulled out
2. power goes out, wind damage
3. freezing cold, hazardous driving conditions
4. flooding, buildings destroyed
5. farmland ruined, people homeless
6. people homeless, wildlife killed
7. crops can't grow, increased risk of wildfires
8. hazardous driving, power out

Page 67
1. positive: looks nicer, can make it exactly the way you want it
   negative: costs money, could take a lot of time, makes a mess
2. positive: hear the music you like

Answer Key, continued

negative: make your brother mad, know you're being inconsiderate
3. positive: have fun with your friends, avoid doing any work
   negative: not helpful, not nice, disappointing parents and grandmother
4. positive: have a new pet, enjoy the parakeet
   negative: costs money, takes time to care for
5. positive: have fun with friend
   negative: really tired next day

Page 68
1. I have to move to the basement because my grandfather is coming to live with us.
2. Because our teacher was sick, the math test was postponed until Monday.
3. Grace's mom got called into work, so Grace had to baby-sit.
4. Blake has a broken leg because he was showing off on his skateboard.
5. Since so many people wanted to buy tickets two more shows were added.
6. We were late for the concert, so we didn't have any dinner.
7. There was a huge snowstorm, so we stayed an extra day.
8. Kate and Kelly stayed up late since there was no school tomorrow.
9. My shoes stuck to the floor because someone had spilled juice on it.
10. Owen ate ten brownies, and as a result, he had a terrible stomachache.

Page 69
1. burning leaves, air pollution, people have trouble breathing, end up in hospital
2. dogs running loose, dangerous, attack people, leash laws
3. oil spill, birds and animals die, cleanup costs much money, people lose jobs

Page 70
1. finding out her report grade
2. They lost the last game of the season. They feel sad.
3. to help them feel better, to end the season on a positive note
4. running around the pool, the floor was wet
5. slip and fall, someone could get hurt seriously, kicked out of pool area

Page 71
1. to protect their heads
2. to get proper nourishment for their bodies to grow and stay healthy
3. to find things easily, to have room to store things
4. to rest, to avoid being tired the next day, to stay healthy
5. didn't do it, student was sick
6. learn more, extra practice, extra credit
7. needs lots of attention, could keep you awake
8. people smile back, everyone feels better, people nicer to you
9. get hungry, tired, cranky
10. tired all day, have more time to get things done during the day

Referents

Page 75
1. automobile
2. shooting hoops
3. salmon
4. birthday present
5. Trey
6. SportsStar shoes
7. cleaning my room
8. vacant lot
9. school concert
10. project

Page 76
1. photographs
2. sun
3. exams
4. Spanish
5. hot chocolate
6. actress
7. zero
8. groceries
9. star formations
10. Florida
11. jeans

Page 77
1. Rachel and Ellie
2. Atlantic Ocean
3. These instruments
4. dairy products
5. Mark Twain
6. Abraham Lincoln
7. the Liberty Bell

Page 78
1. Beautiful flowers
2. Hawaii
3. team sports
4. art supplies
5. Johnson Elementary School
6. Wetlands
7. Tanya

Page 79
1. Luke
2. Haley
3. Luke
4. Luke
5. Kate
6. his history book
7. Kate and Maya
8. *Stranded*
9. boy
10. the burglars
11. Josh
12. his family
13. his mom
14. the burglar with the gold tooth

Page 80
1. our home
2. Charles Dickens
3. people

Answer Key, continued

4. raft
5. Huckleberry Finn
6. Books
7. Reading
8. world

Page 81

1. Lance Armstrong is one of the <u>best cyclists</u> in the world. <u>This world champion</u> has won many bike races all over the world. <u>He</u> is most famous for winning the grueling Tour de France race three years in a row. <u>He</u> is a <u>two-time Olympian</u>. Lance is also a <u>cancer survivor</u>. <u>He</u> beat the odds and is stronger than ever. <u>He</u> has become a <u>role model</u> for all aspiring athletes.
2. Michelle Kwan is a <u>great figure skater</u>. <u>She</u> has skated <u>her</u> way right into the record books. <u>This Queen of the Ice</u> won five straight U.S. championships. <u>She</u> has been named <u>Figure Skater of the Year</u> five times. <u>She</u> has earned more perfect scores in competition than any other skater, male or female. <u>Michelle</u> has won two Olympic medals. <u>This young woman</u> has melted the hearts of <u>her</u> fans.
3. Mia Hamm is <u>a great soccer player</u>. In fact, <u>she</u> is <u>one of the best in the world</u>. <u>She</u> was <u>the youngest player</u> ever to play on the U.S. national team. <u>She</u> won the U.S. Soccer's Female Athlete of the Year award five times. <u>She</u> won a gold medal in the Olympics. <u>The 5'5" forward</u> has used her fame to set up the Mia Hamm Foundation. As <u>spokesperson</u>, one of her goals is to empower young female athletes. <u>She</u> is <u>a great role model</u> for young women.

Page 82

1. Hachiko was <u>Mr. T's dog</u>. <u>She</u> followed (him) to the train station every day when (he) went to work. <u>She</u> met (her master) there every night when (he) came home.

   One evening Mr. T didn't get off the train. Hachiko waited for (the man) all night at the station. People tried to help <u>her</u>, but they couldn't make <u>the poor dog</u> feel better. <u>She</u> didn't understand that Mr. T had died.

   Hachiko went to the train station every night for ten years. People got to know <u>her</u>. They fed <u>her</u>. They took care of <u>Mr. T's faithful companion</u>.

   There is a statue of Hachiko today in the train station so everyone will remember <u>her</u>.

2. Max <u>the mouse</u> was minding <u>his</u> own business in a hotel room. Then the housekeeper came in with (her) vacuum. <u>The little critter</u> dashed under the bed. <u>He</u> hoped [the strong machine] wouldn't come near <u>him</u>. (The busy worker) vacuumed all around, but (she) didn't get to Max. <u>That clever fellow</u> was too far under the bed for [the noisy monster] to grab <u>him</u>. When (the woman) left, Max ran out from <u>his</u> hiding place. "Whew, what a close call!" <u>he</u> sighed with relief.

Page 83

1. Have you ever seen a German shepherd? Maybe you know someone who owns <u>this type of dog</u>. German shepherds are <u>working dogs</u>. <u>These fine animals</u> came from northern Europe many years ago. <u>They</u> have traveled far from <u>their</u> native land where <u>they</u> protected flocks of sheep.

   German shepherds are very brave. <u>They</u> have been used to help police officers catch criminals. In fact, <u>these "police dogs"</u> are so brave that soldiers use <u>them</u> as <u>guard dogs</u>.

   <u>These gentle creatures</u> are very smart and very loyal. That is why <u>they</u> make great <u>Seeing-Eye dogs</u>.

2. Do you know what <u>the largest river in North America</u> is? If you said the Mississippi River, you are right. <u>It</u> is over 2,000 miles long.

   Years ago, when <u>the river</u> was being mapped out, <u>it</u> was called <u>a "gathering of waters."</u> <u>It</u> was also called <u>"Big River"</u> or <u>"Father of Waters."</u> Whatever <u>its</u> name, <u>it</u> is <u>one of the world's most famous rivers</u>.

   <u>This grand body of water</u> has many uses. <u>It</u> is <u>a home for fish and wildlife</u>. <u>It</u> is used for boating and fishing. <u>It</u> is used to transport items on barges.

   Many people enjoy the beauty and history of <u>this great waterway</u> each year.

Page 84

1. a. Molly
   b. a professional singer
   c. a man
2. a. Will
   b. Paul
   c. to understand his math
3. a. Steve
   b. Emma

Answer Key, continued

    c. the party
4. a. Laura and Ellen
    b. Mr. and Mrs. Keene
    c. the school

Page 85
1. a. the bus
    b. the museum
    c. Mr. Price's class
2. a. by the tree
    b. the trail
    c. the boys
3. a. the soccer team
    b. the state championship
    c. the soccer team
4. a. Nate
    b. Mom
    c. the basement

Page 86
1. door
2. man
3. fifth grader (P.J.)
4. cookies
5. aspiring actress (Bree)
6. mitten
7. teacher (Mr. Jones)
8. newspaper
9. principal
10. box
11. Rose
12. baby

Comparing and Contrasting

Page 90
1. walkers, bus riders
2. apartment house
3. Marco Polo, Prince Henry

Page 91
1. skateboard, roller skates
   alike—get places fast, have wheels, can do stunts
   different—wear roller skates, stand on skateboard; skateboard cooler for stunts
2. dorkil, frob
   alike—live on ocean floor
   different—dorkil has silver fins and copper-colored scales, frob is blue and round; dorkil has big mouth and square teeth, frob has small mouth with no teeth; dorkil chases and eats small fish, frob grabs passing small fish with tentacles; frob has no skeleton; frob has tentacles instead of spines

Page 92
alike—sisters, long hair, lived in same apartment
Dot—hair greasy and full of knots, messy, nagging drove her mad
Belle—hair shining and silky, tidy, moved to cleaner place, lived happily ever after

Page 93
Anthony—boy, 14, serious, quiet, wants to be a veterinarian
Silvia—girl, 11, funny and imaginative, wants to be a pilot
both—get along well together, similar personalities, well liked

Page 94
Puffy—red, blue, and black; $125; 1-year warranty; 10 speeds; fuzzy seat
Schween—red, blue, or black; $199.99; 5-year warranty; 21 speeds; good for hilly areas
Answers will vary.

Page 95
alike—tribal, first people on continents, suffered when Europeans came
Aborigines—Australia, don't have reservations, lost traditions
Native Americans—America, live on reservations, practic way of life

Page 96
alike—Australian, enjoy festivals and sports games
outback—sparse population, go to school via radio or mail, rodeos popular
cities—many people, kids walk or ride to school, surfing and sailing popular

Page 97
alike—Answers will vary.
Iroquois—NY/PA area; wigwams or longhouses; fenced villages
me—Answers will vary.

Page 98
alike—superheroes, married, have special powers, fight crime and evil in Metro City, powerful
Zero Man—born on Earth, can disappear and appear, has "truth shield"
Shockra—born on Junga, more powerful, makes electricity and shocks enemies, flies quickly, sees the future

Page 99
Answers will vary.

Page 100
1. tornado, jazz dancer; both twist and turn
2. suitcase, anchor; both heavy
3. fastball, bullet; both travel through the air very quickly
4. prom dress, cloud; both fluffy
5. Blake, clam; keep their mouths closed
6. camels, ships; both used for transportation

Page 101
feet/ice blocks—part of body, frozen water; both very cold
fog/pea soup—water vapor, food; both very thick
heart/stone—human organ, rock; both "hard" (unfeeling)
Kim/bear—girl, animal; both growly, not friendly
sweater/rainbow—clothing, natural phenomenon; both very colorful

Answer Key, continued

Page 102
Answers will vary.

Page 103
alike—walked to school, went to school, morning assignments, worked while teacher busy, helped younger students
Grandma—walked two miles to school, did chores before school, carried lunch bucket, one-room school, only 15 students in school
Celia—walks one mile to school, 30 students in her class, larger school, cafeteria

Fact and Opinion

Page 106
Some flowers aren't very colorful, and (dull flowers are boring.)

Page 107
1. O
2. F
3. F
4. O
5. F
6. O
7. F
8. O
9. F
10. O
11. O
12. O
13. F
14. O
15. F

Page 108
Answers will vary.

Page 109
Reporter: Well, Hank, how many games will the Cats win this year?
Hank Barris: Oh, I don't know. (We'll probably win at least ten.)
Reporter: Wow! (Your fans would be thrilled.)
Hank Barris: You know, we only pulled out three victories last year. (We think we can do better this time around.)
Reporter: How's your arm feeling?
Hank Barris: I had surgery on my elbow last winter. It's getting stronger. (I'll probably come back even stronger this year.)
Reporter: And how about that new contract? (You're making a lot of money for a quarterback on a losing team,) aren't you?
Hank Barris: (It might seem like I'm making way too much money.) The contract says I get paid ten million whether we win or not. Of course, (winning would be better than losing.)
Reporter: Is it true that you're giving a lot of money to charities these days, too?
Hank Barris: (I like to think I'm giving something back to the community.) I do have three foundations that I support.
Reporter: Well, Hank, here's to a great season.
Hank Barris: (We're going to have a lot of fun this year.)

Page 110
1. fact: dries in 5 minutes
   opinion: never need to wait for glorious shine again
2. fact: has 2 chemically balanced ingredients to fight acne
   opinion: gives clearest skin ever
3. fact: spring sale, 25% off
   opinion: no one else offers better selection
4. fact: new store at 2500 W. 176th Street
   opinion: You'll find everything you need at the Trading Post.

Page 111
Answers will vary.

Page 112
facts: 2 hours long; director Martin Carter, begins with Harry starting school; meets a talking stone; reviewer was bored; cast of over 1,000; budget of almost $100,000,000; playing at Valley Green Cinema starting Friday

opinions: movie too long, as horrible as *Triassic Park*, talking stone is a bad idea for a character, the story is boring, people will admire the director for using a huge cast, the costs were a waste of money, viewers won't like the movie

Page 113
Answers will vary.

Summarizing

Page 118
1. Native Americans, desert animals
2. large, live long, food source, grow very slowly
3. southwestern U.S.
4. just before the rainy season
5. They grow very slowly.
6. 30 years
Cross out questions 1, 4, 5, and 6
Summary: The saguaro cactus of the Southwest is special because it's huge, grows slowly, and lives 150 years.

Pages 119-125
Answers will vary.

Answer Key, continued

Inferences

Page 129
1. barely stand still, dream, ticket window, idol, in person
2. table, patted his stomach, napkin, full
3. lap, battle, Number 24, lead, wreck, checkered flag
4. Closed, book, research report, South Branch

Page 130
1. guessed
2. speaker
3. someone who enjoys computers with a passion
4. container
5. disgusted
6. silly, unnecessary
7. pretense, lie, false story
8. avoided, dodged

Pages 131 and 132
Answers will vary.

Page 133
1. underline: numbed up, sting, filling
   occupation: dentist
2. underline: stick to your man, lighting you up, ball, bench, half
   occupation: basketball coach
3. underline: have something you like, red your color, try it on, find other things
   occupation: salesperson
4. underline: order up, over easy, wheat, butter, orders, bacon, table of 16
   occupation: chef, fry cook

Page 134
1. active, attentive to music; always active except when she heard music
2. still active, very musical; many activities, mostly involving music
3. because she has been interested in music all her life
4. Music was something she could do that kept her active when she couldn't leave the house or go to school.

Page 135
1. in a car/van
2. to the movies/concert
3. They're going to sit together, something (show) starts at 8:00.
4. school
5. Devan's homework not being done
6. He keeps forgetting, the assignment book isn't helping, he suggested writing a note on the front of his book.
7. Kate is taking a music lesson.
8. She's been practicing, she has to watch where her fingers go, she's getting the notes right.

Page 136
Answers will vary.

Page 137
1. Yes, because there is no wind or water to disturb them.
2. so astronauts could travel on the moon to see more of it
3. 20 pounds, because the moon's gravity is six times weaker than Earth's gravity.
4. an earthquake on the moon

Pages 138 and 139
Answers will vary.

Page 140
1. school
2. right after lunch
3. grape jelly
4. to see who had eaten anything with grape jelly
5. Ms. Karp didn't realize she had covered the test up with her lunch bag.

Figurative Language

Page 144
1. as fast as the wind; S
2. a rocket; M
3. like an egg; S
4. as gentle as a lamb; S
5. a tank; M
6. as hard as a rock; S
7. a jungle; M
8. an animal; M
9. an oven; M
10. like a stone; S

Page 145
1. Your room is a pigsty; a mess
2. as clean as a whistle; spotless
3. as much as getting his teeth pulled; hates to do it
4. as tall as a mountain; a big pile
5. smelled like a skunk; stank
6. a triangle of cement; hard and dried up
7. as full as a hibernating bear; stuffed

Page 146
1. flew the coop
2. stole the spotlight
3. keep the ball rolling
4. like a glove
5. make heads or tails of it
6. burns me up
7. have a ball
8. sleep on it
9. penny for your thoughts
10. pass the buck

Page 147
1. knock your socks off; impress you
2. nip this thing in the bud; resolve things before they get worse
3. go like clockwork; happen just as it has been planned
4. pulling your leg; teasing you
5. spills the beans; tells the secret
6. out like a light; sound asleep
7. face the music; take responsibility for her behavior

Answer Key, continued

8. barking up the wrong tree; asking the wrong person
9. blew her stack; got very angry
10. beat around the bush; stalled, tried to avoid disclosing the truth

Page 148
1. rain cats and dogs; rain hard
2. pull the wool over your eyes; lie to you to deceive you
3. get back on track; get back to
4. blast off; get started
5. bite the dust; die
   my time is up; my show is over
6. Stay cool; take care, be happy

Page 149
1. b
2. c
3. b
4. c
5. c

Page 150
1. computer screen glared at me; was empty, reminding me I hadn't written the report yet
2. grass tickled the baby's feet; felt soft and active to the baby
3. waves roared; made noise as they crested on the beach
4. chased the rain away; dried up or evaporated the rain
5. the wind screamed; was loud
6. wilted sadly; drooped and bent over or sagged
7. twisted with joy; moved briskly
8. screeched; front door made a noise
9. ran up and down; was moved up and down
10. danced; moved and fluttered

Page 151
1. c
2. a
3. c
4. a
5. b

Page 152
1. a river of tears; many tears, cried hard, cried a lot
2. For the hundredth time; I've already asked you before.
3. ringing off the hook; kept ringing
4. weighs a ton; is very heavy
5. cook an egg on the sidewalk; feels as hot as a frying pan
6. hear a pin drop; was very quiet
7. take me a year; take a long time
8. could explode; I'm really full.
9. find a needle in a haystack; almost impossible
10. size of the Grand Canyon; very large and deep

Page 153
1. a stick of dynamite waiting to go off; metaphor; stressed and ready to vent his emotions
2. as sweet as cotton candy; simile; lovely to hear
3. having my fingernails yanked out; simile, hyperbole; painful
4. moaned and shuddered; personification; made noise as the wind moved them
5. step over the Mississippi River; hyperbole
6. cut to the chase; idiom; quit wasting time, be direct
7. "YOU go fetch the stick!"; personification; I'm too old to chase after sticks.
8. burning a hole in his pocket; idiom; Ian wanted to spend the money right away.

Page 154
true to their name; I
blasted off; I
Becker was a monster; M
Evans was a fiery locomotive; M
lit up the scoreboard; I
the scoreboard shorted out trying to keep up; P
throw in the towel; I
too hot to handle; I
as quick as lightning; S
soared like an eagle; S
The writing was on the wall; I
giving a little cheer; P
hitting the boards; I
It was sweet; I

Page 155
Answers will vary.

Imagery

Page 159
It all started <u>so quietly</u>. <u>Just a few flakes drifted down</u>. The few <u>flakes danced through the air</u> and were <u>joined by many more</u>. Soon the <u>sky was a moving, white wall of snow</u>. The <u>green grass and black streets</u> were <u>slowly covered with fluffy whiteness</u>. Then things became <u>a little less peaceful</u>. The <u>temperature nose-dived</u>. The <u>wind began to whip and swirl</u>. The <u>gentle snow had become a raging blizzard</u>. <u>Gusts of wind drove the tiny bits of snow and ice into windows until they rattled.</u> <u>The air whistled and howled through every crack and into every home.</u> <u>Traffic stopped</u> and <u>people stayed inside</u> to watch and listen.

Page 160
1. over ten feet tall; one large, curly horn sticking up from its head; long, thick tail dragged behind; arms hung nearly to the ground; two foot-long claws; tiny, green eyes; tooth-filled mouth
2. roared; sound no human had probably ever heard
3. felt ground tremble; I licked my lips.
4. smelled like rotten eggs and wet, dirty fur
5. inside of my mouth tasted like metal; tasted like fear

Answer Key, continued

Page 161
Answers will vary.

Page 162
1. stared; huge, square-topped head from side-to-side; studied the big scar that ran down his forehead; touched the metal bolts sticking out from each side of his neck; single tear ran down his cheek
2. sadly; a single tear ran down his cheek

Paragraphs will differ.

Page 163
1. The door to the old house creaked noisily as it slowly swung open. sound
2. As Kendra stepped through the doorway, she pushed away sticky cobwebs that grabbed at her from all directions. touch
3. The old, vacant house smelled dusty and damp. smell
4. Kendra shuddered when she heard a mouse scurry across the floor. sound
5. She was staring at the ghostly shapes of sheet-covered furniture when a hand grabbed her shoulder. touch
6. Kendra screamed like a frightened hyena. sound
7. "Calm down," said Jess, glancing around nervously. sight "It's just me. I found our ball."

Sensory words in paragraph will differ.

Page 164
1. fear
2. relief
3. boredom
4. revenge
5. celebration
6. - 9. Answers will vary.

Page 165
Laura shifted in her chair uneasily. She forced her eyes to stay open. An unexpected yawn made her eyes water. The speaker's boring voice droned on and on, slower and slower, wrapping Laura's ears with soothing, velvet sounds. The warmth of the room seemed to melt her arms and legs into cooked noodles. Laura longed to put her head down and sleep the day away.

Glancing around slowly like an ancient turtle, Laura noticed that several students were struggling to stay awake, some unsuccessfully. Soft snoring reached her drowsy ears. She momentarily rested her head on her arm. Laura nostrils breathed in the scent of pencil erasers, notebooks, and students after PE on a warm day.

Soon Laura's thoughts began to drift away. Her eyelids groaned under their own weight. Before she knew it, Laura had slumped down in her seat and was fast asleep.

Moments later, Laura's body grew restless. Still in a sleep trance, she raised her heavy head from her desk. Her head and one arm fell back and her mouth gaped open like a cave. Laura's papers rustled to the floor as a giant snore escaped from her. She didn't even hear the weak clapping that signaled the end of the speaker's talk.

Page 166
Michael's dark eyes squinted tightly as he walked toward his sister. Anger gripped his body, making his legs stiff and his back ramrod straight. His little sister, Nikki, sat in front of the TV, oblivious to the world around her.

Michael grabbed Nikki's shoulder, sensing the thin, delicate bones hidden beneath her sweater. Surprised, Nikki sucked in her breath and stared at Michael with wide eyes. Michael pushed his face close to hers. He was so close, he could smell peanut butter on her breath and count each freckle on her tiny nose. He noticed she had a small scab on her tiny chin. "She probably fell off her fancy new bike," Michael thought.

"Hey, did you touch my radio?" Michael demanded. Not waiting for an answer, he plowed on like a runaway freight train barreling down a mountain track. "Don't you ever touch any of my stuff again, you got that?" he yelled.

Nikki's soft brown eyes pooled with salty tears. Michael's stomach did flip-flops and his heart melted with understanding. Nikki was only six. "Sorry, Nikki," he said. "I'm just having a bad day. Let's go outside and ride bikes. You take the lead and set the pace." Nikki beamed from ear-to-ear as they headed for the garage.

19-03-98765432

176
Copyright © 2002 LinguiSystems, Inc.

Strategic Learning
Reading Comprehension: Level 2